The English Landscape Garden

A survey

The English
Landscape Garden

A survey

Michael Symes

 Historic England

Published by Historic England, The Engine House, Fire Fly Avenue, Swindon SN2 2EH
www.HistoricEngland.org.uk
Historic England is a Government service championing England's heritage and giving expert,
constructive advice.

The views expressed in this book are those of the author and not necessarily those of
Historic England.

First published 2019
ISBN 978-1-84802-377-2

British Library Cataloguing in Publication data
A CIP catalogue record for this book is available from the British Library.

Brought to publication by Sarah Enticknap, Publishing, Historic England.

Typeset in Georgia Pro 9/11

Edited by Sara Hulse
Indexed by Caroline Jones, Osprey Indexing
Page layout by Hybert Design

Printed in the UK by Gomer Press

Frontispiece
Aerial photo of Wardour [© Historic England Archive 29674/030]

Contents

Acknowledgements

I am indebted to so many garden history friends and colleagues over the years for discussions and their talks and writings on this limitless subject that it would be invidious to name some but not others. That does not, however, imply any lack of deep appreciation. As regards the written word, if I had to single out a book that was ground-breaking in its time and still represents a definitive conspectus, it would be David Jacques' *Georgian Gardens*. In respect of this present book, I am grateful to Michael Cousins for assistance.

Illustrations are from the author's own resources unless otherwise indicated.

Preface

The English Landscape Garden, a garden or park usually on a large scale, is very much a phenomenon of the 18th century, although its legacy can be seen in public parks and in other later developments based on a natural appearance as opposed to a layout founded on geometry and regularity. It was so widespread that even today, when so much has been built over or otherwise changed, one is never far from an example throughout England and much of the more mountainous Scotland or Wales. It also had enormous impact abroad, where the style is often recognised in such terms as 'le jardin anglais' or 'The English Garden', although the Continent had its own traditions of garden-making and, in France and Germany especially, there were contemporary moves towards nature and a natural approach. In addition France looked towards China as a source of inspiration.

Although seemingly natural, the English Landscape Garden was in fact generally the result of considerable contrivance, effort and design skill, the result of 'the art that conceals art'. It might involve digging lakes, raising or levelling hills, and planting trees, sometimes in vast numbers. Nature was arranged and shown to best advantage, often by means of a circuit path or other viewing strategy such as the provision of 'pause seats' that afforded an especially notable view. Its character was determined by the surrounding landscape and topography, which was often brought into the view. Because the landscape itself varies so much within the UK, the resulting appearance of the garden would be mightily different in, say, Yorkshire or Hampshire. Many owners wished the 'Englishness' of the scene to be confirmed by native (or long-established) plantings, although there was a conflict because the extensive importing of species from, in particular, North America gave the more botanically inclined the opportunity to display a far greater range of colour, form and size.

The development of the English Landscape Garden, a gradual process continuing right through the century, was given propulsion by a number of factors, considered in Chapter 1. While most of those relate to local or national interests, and thus corroborate 'Englishness', some came from elsewhere, such as the influence of the Italian *campagna* or paintings of it seen and collected on the Grand Tour.

The English Landscape Garden took many forms, and the variety of manifestations was and remains remarkable. A great number survive, if sometimes in modified form, and can be visited and appreciated. Ways of viewing are varied, from the static point of gazing at scenery to the closer engagement of a circuit, where the visitor experiences the garden as a series of ever-changing 'pictures' and where the visual impact is enhanced by emotional, spiritual and imaginative dimensions.

We may find it difficult today to appreciate just how much of a revolution the landscape garden was, in terms both of garden design and in the perception of what a garden should be; and how much it altered gardens on a global scale. Previously, gardens had been regular and geometrical, with straight canals, clipped hedges and topiary, sculpture and stonework features laid out symmetrically, and trees planted uniformly in avenues. This was the style prevalent in Britain in the early 18th century, based on long traditions in Italian, French and Dutch gardens that were dominant through the Renaissance and baroque eras and beyond.

It is true that the landscape garden had greater significance and importance at the time than it does today, because it occupied a high place in 18th-century life politically, philosophically and culturally: Horace Walpole described it as a sister art to poetry and painting. For that very reason, an understanding of the background and tastes of the time can add to the great obvious pleasures of visiting such a garden today, while appreciation of the associations and mental stimuli that were present can promote reflection as well as immediate enjoyment. Each generation will interpret and respond to the past in its own way, but there will always be food for thought, and additional depth to be gained, by considering the original creation.

Language, or terminology, can sometimes pose a problem. The 18th century used the word 'gardener' to encompass both the manual worker and the designer. This presented a dilemma for Latapie, the French translator of Thomas Whately's *Observations on Modern Gardening* (1770), because 'jardinier', the closest match, meant only the practical gardener in French. 'Lawn' was used freely at the time to describe any stretch or area of grass kept short, and could be far more extensive than the carefully mown modern suburban lawn. Alternatives included 'sward' or 'greensward', and also 'turf', which was used to indicate a covering of grass, usually composed of separate turfs laid down.

The book is structured so as to give the background to, and motivation for, creating the landscape garden; to summarise the chronology of its development; to chart the most significant writers and theorists; and to consider the range of the many forms it took. This last is broadly chronological in dealing with the principal practitioners but it also covers sub-genres of the landscape garden such as the *ferme ornée* and the terrace walk, which are not necessarily confined to a particular period. It may appear that equal weight, in terms of text space, has been given to some aspects that are less significant or less frequently encountered than others, but they may need fuller explanation and include some remarkable and distinctive gardens.

The story of the landscape garden is complex, multilayered and constantly changing in emphasis for such an apparently simple and straightforward construct. It is hoped that this book will help to uncover some of the richness that lies behind a meaningful part of the environment.

1 | The 18th century and the landscape garden

The term 'the English landscape garden' was coined only in the 1940s, but caught on immediately and is widely accepted now as the most convenient and understandable way of expressing the subject in question. Its common use was established in *The English Landscape Garden* by H F Clark (1948). Originally there was no generally accepted term, although William Mason extolled the virtues of the 'English garden' in a poem of that name, while 'landscape gardening' and 'landscape gardener' feature in William Shenstone's *Unconnected Thoughts on Gardening*, published posthumously in 1764. 'The English garden' is ambiguous and needs to be deployed with care, because it is sometimes applied to the entire span of gardens in Britain or has more specialised reference to the later 19th century, where the style was basically naturalistic: Charles Quest-Ritson's *The English Garden Abroad* (1992) concentrates on this later period and scarcely mentions the 18th century.

Conditions in the 18th century were exactly right for the landscape garden to develop and flourish, and it can be seen as a child of its time. The so-called Long 18th Century (approx. 1685–1815) is commonly identified as the Age of Enlightenment, originally concerned with scientific advances and philosophy but later affecting virtually all aspects of life, and certainly gardens, because its twin pillars were reason and nature. Although the Enlightenment was more closely and openly linked with the rise of the landscape garden on the Continent than it was in Britain, nonetheless it can be seen to have had a considerable bearing on developments at home, partly through the pursuit of nature and partly through practical advances made possible by the Agricultural and Industrial Revolutions. The latter, for instance, introduced cast iron for bridges and garden ornamentation. Other advances included botany and botanical nomenclature (the Linnaean system), which boosted international understanding of plants and assisted the growing of exotics. Instruments for surveying and measuring land became more sophisticated and accurate: a recognisable theodolite was introduced in 1720.

A great many factors shaped the progress of the landscape garden, considerations that were 'in the air' at the time. This chapter will attempt to survey the key elements, which varied in importance and application as time went on. Over 40 different factors are presented in summary, but their application will be seen in later chapters dealing with individual gardens. Some of these determining aspects relate to others, but each forms an entity and they are presented here in no special order or priority.

Ideas, motifs and inspirations

A major source of inspiration was the theatre, stretching from Sir John Vanbrugh's mock quasi-theatrical fortifications at Blenheim and Castle Howard at the beginning of the century to Humphry Repton's use of flaps to give 'before' and 'after' views in his Red Books at the end of the century, compared at the time to 'raree' or peep shows. In many designed garden effects there is an element of make-believe that stems from stage scenery. Garden buildings were often put up hastily and flimsily, and pretended to be what they were not (for example wood masquerading as stone).

Some were no more than façades and have been compared to a film set. In the early 17th century Inigo Jones had raised the profile of stage scenery through elaborate settings for masques, and by the early 18th century Sir James Thornhill and others had maintained this tradition. Lord Burlington, as well as being in the vanguard for creating gardens, was a patron of Italian opera, the presentation of which demanded scenery from some of the leading painters of the day. Sometimes the settings were themselves of gardens, and this was one of many inspirations for garden design.

The effects in gardens were two-fold. One was that a particular view might resemble a stage set – Thomas Whately wrote in 1770 of the vista up the cascades from the Palladian bridge at Hagley forming 'a perfect opera scene'. The other was that tangible elements of the theatre were to be found, the most striking being Charles Bridgeman's series of amphitheatres cut in turf, ranging considerably in size up to the magnificent structure at Claremont (*see* Fig 7.5). Elsewhere, the set of triumphal arches in Vauxhall Pleasure Gardens (Fig 1.1) strongly suggested the perspective and wings of a theatre, and indeed was similarly constructed – painted canvas on wood. More generally the use of arches in gardens might owe something to the theatre's proscenium arch. Lord Burlington had the equivalent of an apron stage in front of his Orangery at Chiswick, while tiered planting in shrubberies became known as theatrical planting. On a smaller scale, the wooden display huts with tiered shelving for pots of (originally and mostly) auriculas were called auricula theatres.

Fig 1.1
Triumphal arches at Vauxhall Gardens, London. Engraving by J S Muller after Samuel Wale, 1751.

Fig 1.2 (above)
Fortified wall at Castle Howard.
[© Michael Cousins]

Fig 1.3 (below)
Belvedere at Claremont.
[© Michael Cousins]

Closely connected with the theatre, although manifesting itself in its own way, was military engineering. The use of military-style motifs of fortification and defence earthworks for purposes of (peaceful) garden composition was showy and theatrical. Ideas had come from France in the late 17th century, where the military engineer Vauban turned his attention from war to making the countryside secure in demarcated sections. The devices by which this was achieved were subsequently adopted for garden use. Earthworks would include ramparts, embankments, ditches, earth revetments and bastions, while built fortifications included walls, battlements and towers. Bastions, however, had appeared already, a century or more before. The outstanding exponent in English gardens was Sir John Vanbrugh (1664–1726), himself a former soldier, who built mock fortifications at Blenheim, Oxfordshire, and Castle Howard, Yorkshire (Fig 1.2), plus a number of castellated buildings such as the Belvedere at Claremont, Surrey (Fig 1.3). Stephen Switzer constructed an arrow-headed bastion walk at Grimsthorpe, Lincolnshire, where Vanbrugh had built the house.

Military motifs continued to appear right through the century, by the end of which James Wyatt and John Nash had romanticised them, particularly in respect of castellated houses. Early on, the ha-ha at Stowe, Buckinghamshire, had been studded with stakes driven horizontally into the wall in order to deter the cattle – as if the ha-ha were not completely effective itself. Mock castles appeared post-Vanbrugh at Wentworth Castle, Yorkshire (Stainborough Castle, 1731: Fig 1.4), and especially around mid-century under Sanderson Miller (Radway Grange, Warwickshire; Hagley, Worcestershire; and Wimpole, Cambridgeshire). Bastions were often a feature of the terrace walk (*see* Chapter 11). Some lakes were used for *naumachia* (staged naval battles), as at West Wycombe, Buckinghamshire, or Peasholm Park, Scarborough, and there might be a lakeside fort for the purpose, as at Newstead Abbey, Nottinghamshire (the Byron family seat) or Exton Park, Rutland (Fig 1.5). Even in our own time, Ian Hamilton Finlay created the garden of Little Sparta, south-west of Edinburgh, which bristles with military features and references. It might be added that the Sandby brothers, Paul and Thomas, progressed from military surveying to drawings and watercolours of gardens and landscape, together with some garden architecture.

Fig 1.4 (above)
Stainborough Castle at
Wentworth Castle.

Fig 1.5 (right)
Fort at Exton Park.
[© Michael Cousins]

The perspectives and illusionism of the theatre are comparable to those in paintings, where three dimensions have been reduced to two. The connection between art and gardens was perceived at an early point in the century, with Vanbrugh declaring in 1709 that the ruins of Woodstock Manor, Blenheim, would, if preserved, make 'One of the Most agreable Objects that the Best of Landskip Painters can invent' (Fig 1.6). There was a continual comparison drawn between paintings

Fig 1.6
**Ruins of Woodstock
Manor at Blenheim as
in 1714; print of 1799.**

and garden layout, which was sometimes put to polemical purpose, at its most intense in the Picturesque Controversy of the 1790s. For the whole of the period the connection keeps arising, in different forms. It is important to recognise the ascent of the visual arts during the century, when paintings grew in importance and the status of landscape painting rose within the categories of art. Formal recognition came with the founding of the Royal Academy in 1768. Visual art also received the enormous impetus of wide public circulation through prints.

Illusion could take various forms. At Painshill the lake has often deceived visitors as to its area, including one or two who purported to give an accurate measurement. The lake itself appears from different angles to be, variously, a lake, river or creek. In the same garden the forest to the west gives the impression of being more extensive than its actual size: it was Walpole who climbed the Gothic Tower, looked down and was amazed to find how small it was. At nearby Oatlands, the view from the terrace made the Broadwater (lake) below appear at its extremity to be a river running through the distant Walton Bridge.

The interest in painting was fostered by the Grand Tour, at its height during the 18th century, although punctuated by intermission for war. In addition to seeing scenery of a classical or Renaissance character, often peppered with classical remains, the young *milordi* would also find paintings and sculpture to bring back home.

The paintings were often of landscapes and buildings, the most popular artists being Claude Lorraine, Nicolas Poussin and Gaspard Dughet, with Salvator Rosa adding a wilder, more dangerous note, all from the 17th century, although most sought after in the 18th century. Their reputation and oeuvre spread through the medium of engravings taken from the original paintings. Dutch landscape artists were also often evoked as inspiration and for comparison. A further dimension was provided by Clérisseau and Piranesi, active in Rome at the time, who depicted classical ruins in heightened decay, thus adding a romantic overlay.

Not only were some owners inspired to try to recreate Italianate landscape in their gardens after returning from the Grand Tour (as is commonly said of Stourhead, for instance), but artists who had studied in Rome would sometimes depict gardens and landscape in England in a glow of Italian light, Richard Wilson being the prime example. This was taken to an extreme in Wilson's view of the Ruined Arch at Kew, Surrey (1762: Fig 1.7): until 1949 this was erroneously supposed to represent a feature at the Villa Borghese in Rome.

The relationship between paintings and gardens was sharpened and accentuated by the cult of the Picturesque later in the century. This was a movement pioneered

Fig 1.7
Ruined Arch at Kew,
Richard Wilson, 1762.
[© Gloucester Museums Service]

by William Gilpin (1724–1804) and argued about endlessly in the 1790s by Uvedale Price, Richard Payne Knight and Repton particularly, in which landscape (and by extension gardens and parks) was judged as if it were a painting or series of paintings, and design was based on the principles of painting. Writers on gardens would often cite the names of well-known landscape artists by way of comparison. The concept of the Picturesque was, however, muddied by a growing insistence on wildness, broken shapes and pronounced contrasts as essential to the subject matter that was appropriate in a view. This meant that beauty in regular form or smoothness and harmony, even though present in many a painting, were not fit models for a picturesque landscape.

Another guiding aesthetic principle was that of the serpentine line, the 'Line of Beauty'. Popularised by Hogarth in mid-century, the wavy line affected many of the visual arts. In gardens, early application saw intricate rococo windings of paths or streams, while broader, more gentle undulations are often perceived to underlie the contouring of Brown's parks and the shape of his lakes.

Nature lay at the heart of the landscape garden. It was a key concern and matter for debate among thinkers of the Enlightenment in Britain and on the Continent, an early disquisition coming from the 'Philosopher Earl' of Shaftesbury, whose work *The Moralists* (1709) proclaimed not just the glory of nature but its virtue: 'O GLORIOUS *Nature*! supremely Fair, and sovereignly Good! All-loving and All-lovely, All-divine! Whose Looks are so becoming, and of such infinite Grace; whose Study brings such Wisdom, and whose Contemplation such Delight.'

The first half of the 18th century was known as the Augustan Age, with reference to the classical arts supposedly reaching their apogee in the reign of the Emperor Augustus. This echo indicates in itself the esteem in which the ancient world and the classics were held, together with the perceived need at the time to emulate them and seek the authority and precedent of the classics when creating new works. Myths and classical figures were thus frequently the subject matter of plays, operas and other literary works. And when gardens exhibited literary allusions (such as Stowe or The Leasowes), usually through inscriptions, most were quotations from Roman authors or references to familiar myths or tales. The Augustan Age also implied what was actually the case, that it was a predominantly literary time. Aspects of the 'new gardening' were accordingly developed among the writers and thinkers (*see* Chapter 3), and tended to appear in print before they were properly implemented on the ground. However, there was a marked change during the middle years of the century, when the stock of painting as an art grew and the focus switched somewhat to the visual arts. This of course aided the fortunes of the landscape garden and encouraged those who wished to relate gardens to painting. Gardens became less cerebral, although there was still much to occupy the mind through associations (usually more general where they had earlier been specific).

The swing from the written word to the visual arts, and also a change in attitude towards the classical world, can be illustrated by the specific case of the Greek Revival from around 1760. This was occasioned by expeditions to Greece and the Middle East, beyond the normal boundaries of the Grand Tour, to excavate sites of Greek architecture and bring back measured drawings. There was considerable interest in these findings, and Greek buildings began not to be copied exactly but to inspire creative and decorative design, as in the case of Robert Adam. No longer was the classical world a necessary precedent, but a source to be exploited alongside other sources. In gardens the Greek Revival produced a new generation of buildings, particularly at Shugborough, Staffordshire (Fig 1.8), Hagley (Fig 1.9) and West Wycombe, Buckinghamshire.

Several of the expeditions were sponsored by the Society of Dilettanti, set up in 1732 for the benefit of those who had been on the Grand Tour and who wished to further their study of the classical world (meaning Italy originally), although it also had the reputation of a heavy drinking club. A proportion of members of the Dilettanti were interested in developing their own landscape gardens, and ideas and knowledge would circulate among them, resulting in one or two garden buildings (the Temple of Theseus at Hagley and the Tower of the Winds at West Wycombe) appearing before the publications bearing illustrations of the Greek originals had come out.

There was an emphasis on the role of the imagination in responding to scenery that continued right through the period. Joseph Addison spoke of the pleasures of imagination as he proceeded through the walks and meadows at Magdalen College, Oxford, and it is clear that visitors were expected to respond likewise to the associations triggered by what they saw in a garden. In a formal garden it would probably be a named building, a sculpture or an inscription: in a landscape garden the imagination would, for instance, follow a lake as it wound out of sight, or bring to life a ruin and its original envisaged occupants.

Taste was all-important in the 18th century, and there could be no greater accolade than to describe someone as possessing fine taste. But taste could,

Fig 1.8
Hadrian's Arch, Shugborough.

Fig 1.9
Temple of Theseus at Hagley.

and did, change, particularly as it was so subjective and a matter of opinion, even if claimed to be based on objective standards. The most striking example would be mountainous scenery, such as would be encountered in Wales, Scotland and the Lake District. Early in the century mountains were often regarded as 'God's rubbish' and undesirable to visit. But Gilpin and others turned that on its head, so that from about 1750 these areas were described enthusiastically, opened up and tourism was encouraged. The relationship between taste and passing fashion was often debated: George Mason, attacking Thomas Whately's *Observations on Modern Gardening* (1770), accused the author of mistaking fashion for taste, and said Whately's opinions would need to be altered every year.

One important factor that coloured the appearance of the landscape garden was 'Englishness'. Although sentiments would differ, patriotism was particularly high at times of war (such as the Seven Years' War against France) and also as recognition of the standing the country had as a naval power, a leader in technology and in its steady expansion of empire. Its constitution – governed by Parliament, with a limited monarchy – was admired abroad, especially, it might be said, by reformists in France. Englishness was expressed in a number of ways in the garden. First, the 'natural' look embraced and portrayed the English countryside. Second, the plantings in some gardens were deliberately restricted to native or what were regarded as traditional species. Third, the plainness of a typical Brown park can be seen as reflecting what has been taken to be part of the English character – straightforward, to the point, no nonsense, no frills. This had found much earlier expression in the *parterre à l'Angloise* in formal gardens, a simple grass plat as opposed to the elaborate embroidered parterres of the French and Dutch. Fourth, inclusion of Gothic buildings and ruins (both real and sham) harked back to a native past.

Part of the drive towards expressing Englishness and traditional culture lay in looking to the past. The Grand Tour, which revealed so much of ancient splendours in the countries visited, encouraged those at home to seek out as much as they could that was comparable. The Society of Antiquaries was founded in 1717, and under its auspices archaeology became a serious science. The eccentric William Stukeley was a leading figure, who conducted pioneering work on Stonehenge and Avebury, but drew misguided conclusions. He believed both were Druidic, in accordance with his lifelong obsession with the subject. In regard to gardens, he was an early exponent of both Gothic and Druidic elements, with his Grantham garden (from 1726) being focused on a 'Druidic grove', planted in concentric circles like Stonehenge, but with filberd trees in place of stones, and centred on an old apple tree garlanded with sacred mistletoe. His final garden, in Kentish Town, London, begun at the age of 73, was a small plot that in essence was a hermitage garden with a long, curving 'Druidic Walk' of grass with flowering shrubs sown in it. In the fanciful application of supposed Druidic motifs by Stukeley and others one can see prescient stirrings of romanticism. Several henges sprang up, such as at Park Place, Henley (Fig 1.10).

Looking at the past was also very much a political matter. The 18th century had a curious, rather vague, view of the span of bygone eras, and consequently the Ancient Britons, King Alfred and then the medieval age were often blurred together, sometimes deliberately if it suited political purpose. The rule of the Druids over the Ancient Britons was viewed as benevolent and

Fig 1.10
The Druid's Altar at Park Place, Henley. Engraving by George Cooke after William Alexander, 1817.

tolerant, and based on liberty (despite such unfortunate elements as human sacrifice), which is the crucial principal political philosophy of the century and one that was seen as underpinning garden design. King Alfred was revered for his innovations in justice and fairness, such as trial by jury. Likewise, the world of medieval Gothic (considered, although incorrectly, as a native architectural style) was regarded as embodying liberty in the form of Magna Carta. So the Whig opposition (to Sir Robert Walpole's Whig administration), which grew from 1733 and eventually came to power, championed liberty – and this could be expressed by the use of Gothic garden buildings, although after 1750 deployment of this style became more fanciful, rococo and usually just decorative.

Politics had both a party and a national dimension. On the international stage, France was the principal enemy and the subject of satire and derision (notably by Hogarth). This surfaced in comparison of the 'free' landscape garden with the formal gardens of Louis XIV, whose absolute monarchy was seen to be reflected in the tyranny over nature in strict and regular layouts.

One strain of 'Englishness' which was seized on, particularly by the French, for being characteristic was melancholy. This element had been identified with the English at least as far back as the Elizabethan age, when the four 'humours' said to constitute a person were made much of, for example in Ben Jonson's play *Every Man in his Humour*. Melancholy was associated with meditation in the garden or contemplation of the landscape at large. Features such as ruins in the garden were calculated to produce a 'pleasing melancholy'. Sometimes the French devised their gardens as an arena for socialising, in deliberate contrast to what they saw as the tendency to enjoy an English garden alone for contemplation.

England did not have a monopoly on nationalistic thoughts. The Welsh and Scots had bardic traditions that spoke of their own military past, glorified and romanticised. Thomas Gray's poem *The Bard* (1757) was illustrated by Thomas Jones, showing the wild and windswept old bard proclaiming defiance in a setting of Welsh mountains with a henge close by. The bards were seen as preserving Druidic traditions, hence the henge. In Scotland the cult of Ossian spread through Europe, evoking an ancient Celtic or Gaelic world, supposedly based on a cache of old poems but mostly if not entirely manufactured by James Macpherson in the 1760s. There was also pointed reference, after the Jacobite rising and its subsequent defeat at Culloden in 1746, to the triumph over the Scots in the form of garden buildings, prominently at Virginia Water, Surrey, bestowed on the Duke of Cumberland (the 'butcher of Culloden') by a grateful monarch (his father, George II).

A source of contention to the present day is the possible influence of Chinese gardens. Some authors wrote of irregular Chinese layouts, Sir William Temple having spoken of their *sharawadgi* (novelty, surprise, variety) as early as 1685, but visual representations (such as those on lacquerwork and fabrics, and sometimes engravings) were so stylised and remote from English topography that they could hardly have served as a model. William Chambers, who was highly regarded on the Continent if not at home, pushed the Chinese cause as hard as he could, inventing much of it, and was believed by the French, who in consequence dubbed it 'le jardin anglo-chinois', much to the indignation of Horace Walpole and several other English commentators.

Combining the productive with the pleasurable and aesthetic was a venerable idea, going back at least as far as the Romans. Garden and farm elements had always coexisted on an estate, but their relationship came to a head in the 18th century. In the previous century a feeling had been growing that features such as fields and meadows (and therefore part of designed agricultural areas) were in themselves attractive, which led to attempts to integrate farm and garden more closely. This developed into Switzer's 'farm-like way of gardening' and the *ferme ornée* (*see* Chapter 11).

Economics played a part as well. The old elaborate formal gardens were demanding and labour-intensive, whereas, although large sums might be needed to set up a landscape garden, once established it would be considerably cheaper to maintain. Sheep would be the principal gardeners and keep the grass admirably short and pleasant to look at and walk on, with cattle and deer also contributing. Such maintenance as was required, for fences and ha-ha walls, was relatively low in cost.

Dynasty was an important factor in terms of planting. Most landscape gardens were, by virtue of their scale alone, the preserve of the aristocracy who held and controlled so much of the land. At the time, aristocratic family dynasties, some of which had already been in existence for centuries, would be regarded as permanent, with the expectation that the estate would be handed down to the next generation. So, although in creating a landscape garden the owner and designer would generally keep and incorporate existing mature trees, there would inevitably be considerable planting of young trees that would only reach maturity decades later, perhaps even a century later. It was a case, therefore, of planting for posterity.

Garden buildings had more impact in the 18th century than at any other time in terms of range, style and energy in the overall propulsion of the garden. The effects could be aesthetic, stimulating in evoking associations, or appealing to those with a connoisseur's interest in architecture. As a garden building was so much less costly to erect than a house, it meant that experiments in architecture could be conducted without too much risk or investment. All the leading architects of the day turned their hand to garden buildings, sometimes termed follies, and although many ephemeral works (some of dubious quality) were produced, there were equally many which left the greatest memory of a garden. The role of a garden building could range from purely decorative to ornamental but functional and to iconographic (*see* Chapter 6).

Geometry had underpinned the design of formal gardens for centuries, and although it might not be visible or immediately apparent in the landscape garden, alignments that produced vistas and views were common and indicated a high degree of sophistication on the drawing board, as well as a keen eye in the landscape itself.

Specialised religious or interest groups played a significant part in aspects of the garden. Quakers were prominent in botany and the cultivation and collection of plants, the justification being that the wide (global) range of plants proclaimed God's bounty and served to raise wonder and admiration for them as God's work. In another sphere Freemasonry (which shared many of the ideals of the Enlightenment) expressed itself in symbolism in gardens, although, it has to be said, far less so in Britain than in Continental Europe, where garden buildings are known to have contained masonic imagery or been used for masonic ceremonies.

Practicalities

In addition to ideas and cultural factors, there were several usages and operational advances in the garden that affected maintenance and appearance. A predominant element was plantings, which will be covered in more detail in Chapter 10, but it can be registered now that the import of exotic species at an ever-increasing rate through the century led to radical change in the composition, and hence in the appearance, of many landscape gardens. Not every owner found this desirable, however, as we have already seen. There were also practical and political dimensions in growing timber, the first to manage woodland for commercial purposes and the second to satisfy the navy's constant demand for shipbuilding material. The case for growing trees for the nation had been forcefully proposed by John Evelyn in his classic treatise *Sylva* (1664).

Older and existing features in a garden, harking back to formal times, were often modified to play an appropriate role in a landscape garden. Thus, although there was plenty of earth moving, digging and planting, older elements, whether of landform or built, might survive, perhaps in modified form. Grand formal avenues of trees, such as at Wimpole or Blenheim, might be not just left but replanted when the original trees came down. The intricate winding paths of the formal wilderness led to the sinuous waving rococo shapes in the 'artinatural' garden (*see* Chapter 5). Mature trees, particularly those of significant size or beauty, would be preserved and form the basis of designed woodland areas, to avoid having plantations only of saplings. Brown, among others, did devise a means for moving mature trees, however, although this did not always succeed and was not carried out on any great scale. Similarly, existing garden buildings were often left, although they might be gradually slimmed down, as at Stowe. And when a landscape garden was imposed on a previous large formal garden, as frequently happened, the structural vestiges of the earlier layout might still be apparent.

Land was the most important factor of all. A relatively small number of aristocratic owners held vast acreages, which facilitated landscaping and park-making on a scale that shrank considerably in future centuries. Many of these owners owed their wealth to sugar, in other words the slave trade in the West Indies. Some entrepreneurs and private citizens, such as William Beckford at Fonthill, Wiltshire, could own or acquire large estates, but changes in society after 1800 led to the rise of the suburban garden and in gardening as a national hobby. In consequence gardens began to be considered in very different ways.

Enclosure had a profound effect on the extent of land being turned over to park or landscape garden. In almost all cases an Act of Parliament was required for a landowner to take over what previously had been common land or farmed in strips by tenant farmers. Enclosure had been practised for centuries but gathered momentum from about 1760 and was at its peak for the next half century.

Improvements in roads and in the suspension and comfort of carriages led to an increase in garden visiting, so that the pleasures and appearance of a landscape garden could be more widely disseminated. This went hand in hand with a proliferation of guidebooks, topographical texts and prints of gardens, all spreading the word and establishing the taste for the new gardening.

The Agricultural Revolution, encompassing rotation of crops, animal breeding and more efficient ways of working the soil, whether arable or pasture, led to greater economy and productivity. It was spread over a long time, and was a subject of considerable concern and interest, as reflected in the work of the Society of Improvers in the Knowledge of Agriculture in Scotland and in the popularity of agricultural writers such as William Marshall and Arthur Young. Advances in implements, which had mostly remained the same for centuries, included Jethro Tull's seed drill, for example. Britain became a beacon for practical progress, and visitors from abroad would come as much to learn about agricultural improvement as they did to seek out new ideas for laying out gardens. What the revolution achieved in practical terms was matched by changes in the appearance of land, whether actively farmed or grazed park. It also resulted in the creation of model farms with functional buildings that were architect-designed and thus added to aesthetic appeal.

The Industrial Revolution furthered agricultural progress by the introduction of new machinery, while cast iron added to decorative possibilities. Russia was quick to take up the processes of casting iron, as the startling arch at Tsarskoye Selo indicates (Fig 1.11). Some gardens actually made the processes themselves picturesque, such as Warmley, Gloucestershire, where the furnaces were built into a series of grottoes. Cinders and burnt slag left over from manufacture contributed widely to decoration of grottoes and rustic structures.

Usage determined design to some extent. In addition to a rise in hay meadows to cope with the increase in keeping and breeding horses, patches of lawn would have to be level enough for the burgeoning pastime of cricket (which led to the death of Frederick, Prince of Wales, who is said to have been weakened by a cricket injury sustained in the grounds at Cliveden, Buckinghamshire). It might be thought that field sports – hunting and shooting – would be a substantial factor, but it is debatable whether the changes in hunting practice or shooting techniques (with lighter guns) had much effect, on Brown's parks at least. Some of these changes were not introduced until after Brown's time. On the other hand, some traditional design elements shaped by deer hunting, such as clear avenues between woodland, survived from formal times. The keeping of deer diminished in proportion to the great increase in sheep and cattle.

The ha-ha, so instrumental in making a seamless transition from garden to park and in calling in the country, is firmly associated with Brown's layouts, but its roots were in the formal garden of more than 50 years before. The device was of French origin, as described in D'Argenville's *La Théorie et la Pratique du Jardinage* of 1709, where it is called an 'Ah' to indicate the gasp of surprise upon unexpectedly discovering it at one's feet. It appeared at Levens Hall, Cumbria, in the 1690s and was popularised by Charles Bridgeman, for example at Stowe (Fig 1.12), where it remains, although straight. It proved ideal for the later landscape garden, providing a distant view of the countryside and making it appear part of the garden, while fulfilling the practical function of keeping cattle or other livestock out of the garden.

Lawn (grass, turf) was the single largest component of the landscape garden and, thanks to the British climate, it could reach the highest standards of finish, making it the envy of Continental Europe, which was often too hot and dry for grass to flourish. Close attention was paid to types of grass, as well as how to maintain it (sheep or labourers). Brown's favourite was clean hay seed mixed with Dutch clover.

Fig 1.11
Iron arch at Tsarskoye Selo, Russia.

Fig 1.12
Straight ha-ha wall at Stowe.

Lakes, at their zenith during the 18th century, were the centrepiece of the majority of gardens, and this was especially true of Brown. His early reputation was that of a water engineer, and he achieved prodigious results – such as draining a swamp at Croome (Fig 1.13). New lakes, if the ground was porous, would require a puddled clay lining: climate and situation would also be a factor. Clay was also used for reinforcing banks and as a core, sometimes a blanket, for dams and cascades. The spoil from excavating lakes was often used to raise artificial hillocks (as at Kew) and thus vary the landform.

Fig 1.13
Lake with grotto at Croome Court.

Paths could vary from sand or plain soil tracks to low-cut grass. However, the favoured composition was gravel, which constituted an unmistakeable indication of the route to be taken, even across parkland. Thomas Whately (1770) claimed that gravel paths were the sign of a garden and that their use in a park conferred on the park the air of a garden, as at Hagley. Brown's use of gravel paths was sometimes condemned by those who thought it detracted from the 'natural' appearance. Gravel was associated with the English landscape garden, although introduced much earlier, and Catherine the Great, for one, became 'gravel mad' in her eagerness to employ it in Russian gardens.

2 | The evolution of the landscape garden

This chapter attempts to summarise chronologically the ways in which the landscape garden developed and changed across the 18th century. It is no more than a skeleton that will be fleshed out in later thematic chapters or those concerned with individual designers.

The landscape garden evolved gradually and did not take any single form. Indeed, it displayed a remarkable range of types and appearances, often linked to the local topography. At different periods there would be a different emphasis on one aspect or another, and it can be seen that a pivotal figure such as Kent or Brown focused interest and taste on their own identifiable approach to garden-making, which then spread widely. It should also be said that the landscape garden was mainly in the hands of wealthy landowners with large tracts of land at their disposal, and that smaller gardens, from the 'squirearchy' and middle class to town gardens, might remain regular until the end of the 18th century. Furthermore, a regular formation was often the most efficient, not only to grow fruit and vegetables (usually within a walled garden) but to display flowers.

The situation in 1700 was that large gardens were almost entirely formal in the Dutch and French traditions, but the series of bird's-eye views by Kip and Knyff of that period indicate occasional paths winding through woodland and an awareness of the countryside beyond. In addition to the attraction of views of that countryside, an aesthetic appreciation of closer effects that were naturalistic in appearance – woods, fields, streams – had grown during the 17th century, often within the context of agricultural or farm land. Timothy Nourse's *Campania Foelix* of 1700 has a frontispiece of parterres juxtaposed with an image of a horse and plough, and although we are not yet at the stage of the *ferme ornée*, nonetheless the idea of yoking the ornamental to the agricultural, the pleasurable to the productive, would gather considerable momentum.

The idea that nature itself was attractive and desirable led to a reaction initially against some of the excesses of artificiality in gardens, such as topiary clipped into fantastical shapes. The garden itself remained regular for the time being, but it became more and more important to incorporate views of what lay outside. At first this was tentative, Walpole describing how Charles Bridgeman 'dared to introduce cultivated fields, and even morsels of a forest appearance, by the side of those endless and tiresome walks' in Richmond Gardens. The pace quickened, with Pope advocating 'calling in the country' and Switzer expanding the designer's outlook to extensive, rural or forest gardening (*see* Chapter 4). Meanwhile, from about 1715, changes were afoot even within the formal garden, with wiggles in the groves adjacent to straight walks – what Batty Langley described as the 'artinatural' garden (*see* Chapter 5).

What 'nature' meant in the 18th century may be something rather different to what we might think it means today – and indeed the word had changing implications over the course of the century. When some authors (*see* Chapter 3) used 'nature' early on, it appears that, in regard to garden design, it meant allowing trees and topiary to grow unclipped and to develop without uniform pruning even within regular planting patterns. Alexander Pope mocked the excesses of topiary, but his own small garden at Twickenham was mostly regular, although some asymmetrical compartments were introduced. When he announced, in reference to his grotto, 'Approach! Great Nature studiously behold', he alluded to the stones and minerals that were sent to him by friends and which decorated the walls of the grotto. The point was that Pope was proud of the fact that the pieces in question had not been cut or polished in any way – they were in their 'natural' state.

There can be confusion in 'nature' or 'natural' covering both a garden's appearance and the fact that nature's materials – plantings, grass, water – are present equally in formal gardens. The many references to, and comparisons with, landscape paintings that we have come across in the previous chapter may give the impression that landscape gardens in a naturalistic form were more advanced on the ground than they actually were. William Kent is often regarded as the founder of the 'natural style', yet there was much that was regular and geometrical in his work. It was Horace Walpole who said that under Kent, 'Freedom was given to the forms of trees; they extended their branches unrestricted', although he also criticised him for creating 'puny' clumps intended for immediate effect not futurity, and declared that the clumps on the lawn at Euston Hall, Suffolk, resembled the ten of spades. The natural look as we would conceive it would come later, and by the time of Brown, whose landscapes were praised (and sometimes censured) for appearing natural, in fact it was a carefully arranged and idealised nature. True unspoiled nature, although sometimes given a helping hand, only came fully with the Picturesque in the later part of the century.

Switzer encouraged what he called 'the farm-like way of gardening', combining the practical needs of running a farm with the aesthetic pleasures of a designed garden, and indeed attempting to integrate the two by bringing ornament into the fields and into the view of them. In the footsteps of Switzer, the *ferme ornée* gathered strength, from early essays in the late 1710s and 1720s to The Leasowes in mid-century (*see* Chapter 11).

One of the principal engines for calling in the country was the ha-ha, as mentioned in Chapter 1, a sunken ditch with a revetment wall on the home side and an incline up to the field outside. Invisible from the house until one came right up to it, it provided an apparently seamless transition from garden to park or farmland, and also served the practical purpose of preventing cattle from straying into the garden. The device was installed in Britain early on when gardens were still formal, notably under Bridgeman, as can be seen today with the straight examples at Chiswick or Stowe (*see* Fig 1.12). Later the possibilities became apparent for, in effect, merging park and garden, as Brown was to do, and curving or irregular ha-has are to be found in many a landscape garden.

William Kent (*see* Chapter 7) exploited the ha-ha in his efforts to give the landscape garden a new direction. What he established from *c* 1730 was the idea of the garden as a pictorial circuit, moving from one building or other feature to the next, with cumulative effect. How different from the old formal gardens with their goose-foot allées, where the visitor would have to decide which path to take from a choice of maybe three or five. Kent's well-preserved masterpiece is at Rousham, where an intricate circuit affords surprises, set pieces and a balance between internal and external views. Kent was praised for his 'naturalness', but although he opened up gardens and 'saw that all nature was a garden', his work, as has been said, was never entirely free from regularity. It has to be remembered that the landscape garden was a slow revolution, and that new irregular plantings would often go along with old trees allowed to remain in formal patterns but progressively unclipped.

Clearly landscape gardening was also a matter of fashion, and developments would spread as owners endeavoured to keep up with their neighbours. As a result, certain parts of the country would boast enclaves or clusters of gardens contributing to, and reflecting, the character of the whole area. Thus the great West Midlands trio of Hagley, Enville and The Leasowes flourished and grew from the 1740s, inspired by each other. The spirit of competition might provoke local rivalries, such as between Wentworth Castle and Wentworth Woodhouse, South Yorkshire. The 'five fine Surrey gardens' formed a close crescent (Claremont, Esher Place, Oatlands, Painshill, Woburn Farm), dating from the 1730s onwards as landscaped gardens. The area around Richmond and Twickenham was known as 'Twickenhamshire', a cultural community of villas and gardens reaching down to the Thames and which included such distinguished inhabitants as Pope and Horace Walpole.

Some of the greatest of 18th-century gardens came into being in mid-century – circuit gardens inspired by Kent but going much further in terms of scope and natural appearance. These included Shugborough, Stourhead, Painshill, Kew, West Wycombe, Hestercombe, Halswell and Wotton (Buckinghamshire), together with several of the great Yorkshire estates. The emphasis on visual, pictorial experience, combined with mood, character and atmosphere, points to a move from the intellectual/cultural associations of the formal garden to something that appealed more to the heart and the eye. This was reflected, too, in a decline of the need to see the classical world as providing an essential cultural basis and precedent. The importance of an emotional response to the landscape garden was summed up by Thomas Whately in 1770, when he described the pictorial garden as 'expressive', in contrast to earlier gardens with specific cultural references, which were 'emblematic'.

In mid-century too there was a fashion for small-scale gardens of an intricate, irregular and sometimes wilful and playful kind, which has been called rococo. This fits in with the pictorial circuit, although not with the expansiveness of landscape. Painswick Rococo Garden, Gloucestershire, with its asymmetry of paths and idiosyncratic architecture (Fig 2.1) is the best surviving example; others, now lost, are to be found in the delightful watercolours of Thomas Robins.

In gardens this change in sensibility from around 1750 assumed two contrasting forms. One was the Brownian park, epitomised in the work of 'Capability' and his many followers. Garden and park merged, often via a ha-ha, and although Brown himself and architects such as Adam and Chambers might add garden buildings, there was generally less emphasis on them in the impetus to create an open, natural-looking landscape. The alternative form was the continuation and refinement of the pictorial mode, relying heavily on the idea of the circuit and a sequence of set scene 'incidents', usually a building but, as time went on, increasingly features such as cascades. The pictorial, building-studded gardens flourished until at least the 1770s, when the number of buildings started to decrease.

The difference between the Brownian park and the pictorial garden was not just a matter of physical appearance. It was also the way of viewing the garden. In many of Brown's landscapes it would be sufficient

Fig 2.1
The 'hinged' Red House at Painswick. [© Michael Cousins]

for the owner and his friends to admire from the house the long views that had been opened up, without having to walk or ride into the landscape, although that would of course have been desirable. Often the view from the house was the 'key' one. With the circuit garden, however, it was vital to engage with the landscape and experience the variety of visual and emotional elements in sequence and at close hand. More intimate, sometimes enclosed, effects were therefore possible. Another important difference was that the house was the centre or focus of the landscape in a Brown park, just as it had been in the earlier formal garden, whereas in many pictorial gardens such as Stourhead, Hestercombe or Painshill, the layout was self-contained and did not relate to the house, which was often out of sight.

A feature of many a Brown design was the belt of woodland around the perimeter of an estate. So far from opening up to the countryside, as had been the overall tendency of the landscape garden thus far, it actually emphasised the boundaries of the property and acted as a barrier, visual and physical, against the wider landscape. Humphry Repton, against opposition, approved – and bestowed the word 'appropriation' on marking an owner's boundary when recommending it to a client.

Variety was another major difference. Architecture or other set piece features exerted considerable appeal, and at the time there were more visitors to pictorial gardens than there were to Brown sites, as the journals of, for example, travellers from the Continent attest. George Mason, writing in 1798, in the second Appendix to his *An Essay on Design in Modern Gardening* of three years earlier, stated that: 'The works of HAMILTON [Painshill] and SHENSTONE [The Leasowes], and of *many more voluntary artists*, were *generally* preferred by the public to those of any *professor* in the art.' Professor meant professional, with obvious reference to Brown. There is a significant difference between a garden designed by a professional such as Brown who produced a plan and an owner who had an original, imaginative and evolving vision. A plan is intrinsically static, although of course it can be modified and altered over the years in practice; but an owner had the advantage of experiment, change and response to trends in garden design.

The Picturesque tended in the direction of the wild or Sublime, with its currency of mountains, rocks, cataracts and precipices. William Gilpin, traditionally hailed as the father of the Picturesque, said the subject always stirred his mind to thoughts of the sort of scenery to be encountered in the Lake District, where he spent his childhood. This led to some landscapes being left as far as possible in their natural state, as Richard Payne Knight and Uvedale Price attempted to do – or said that was the case. The two illustrations in Knight's *The Landscape* (Figs 2.2 and 2.3) show, in exaggerated form, the difference between a landscape 'dressed' by Brown or his followers and the same scene as unspoiled by any art or interference (sometimes Fig 2.3 has been mistaken for a landscape deliberately rendered picturesque). Knight's poem plus Price's *An Essay on the Picturesque* provoked the Picturesque Controversy, which raged for a decade or so before becoming the subject of mockery.

Humphry Repton, taking up the baton from Brown, was somewhat torn between a general adherence to Brownian principles, a taste for the Picturesque and a strong obligation that he felt towards pleasing the client. This meant providing as much 'convenience', as he called it, as possible for the owner. Setting up as a landscape gardener in 1788, five years after Brown's death, he endeavoured to fill the gap at the top, because none of the many Brown followers and successors seemed to have quite that stature. It is sometimes claimed that the term 'landscape gardener' was coined by Repton but, as mentioned earlier, it appears in Shenstone's *Unconnected Thoughts on Gardening* a quarter of a century before.

Fig 2.2 (above)
A landscape 'dressed' in Brownian style. Etched by Benjamin Pouncy after Thomas Hearne, from Richard Payne Knight, *The Landscape*, 1794.

Fig 2.3 (above right)
A landscape untouched. Etched by Benjamin Pouncy after Thomas Hearne, from Richard Payne Knight, *The Landscape*, 1794.

Although Repton stated in his various writings that his principles of design did not change during his career, which lasted for more than 25 years, in fact it can be seen that he moved more and more in the direction of a rather cosy 'Villa Picturesque', in which varied compartments such as flower gardens were concentrated near the house, as at Ashridge or Endsleigh, contrasting with the more naturalistic and occasionally wilder park beyond. Sometimes he would follow Brown at a site and modify the plantings, thinning out where they had grown too large and dense.

If the great change in sensibility from head to heart in mid-century resulted in new perceptions of the garden, then an equally seismic change occurred towards 1800. The elements of imagination and emotion so dear to earlier writers were lost, and a pleasing appearance was all. By concentrating more and more on ornamental gardening, Repton was not only signalling a general change in taste and sensibility but also a loss in the standing of garden design. From his time onwards, it would not be possible to claim for it the high status it had earlier enjoyed, fuelled by philosophy and politics. Gardening was starting to become more practical and feasible, and would become a widespread interest among the burgeoning and often suburban middle classes. Repton maintained that he followed William Mason, who had spoken of composing landscape 'with a poet's feeling and a painter's eye' but manifestly concentrated on the latter, leaving the Lake Poets of the 1790s, Wordsworth and Coleridge, to invest the viewing of scenery with poetry.

Although there were far fewer buildings around the turn of the century, and into the 19th, those architects who designed them, and usually the house too, such as the Wyatts (including Wyatville) and John Nash, tended to produce more decorative work, certainly in comparison with the sometimes rather austere classicism or Gothicism to be encountered in the earlier 18th century. This can be seen as in tune with the late Picturesque and romanticism, and would lead in time to the much smaller-scale decorative suburban garden.

3 | Theorists and writers

The status of gardens and garden design was higher in the 18th century than at any other time before or since. The leading poets and writers of the time turned their attention to the subject, and Alexander Pope declared that 'Gardening is near-akin to Philosophy' and also that 'Gardening is more Antique & nearer God's own Work, than Poetry' – 'gardening' in the 18th century covering both design and physical labour, as mentioned. One of the greatest Prime Ministers of the century, William Pitt the Elder, was a considerable garden-maker in his own right, apart from having a deep and informed knowledge of the subject. And when Lord Poullet wrote in 1749 that Charles Hamilton of Painshill '(now that Mr Kent is dead) is certainly ye top man of taste in England' he did not qualify it by adding 'in gardens'.

The standing of the landscape garden was a matter of considerable pride. Thomas Whately opened his 1770 treatise by declaring that 'Gardening, in the perfection to which it has lately been brought in England, is entitled to a place of considerable rank among the liberal arts', while Walpole, writing at around the same time, proclaimed that 'Enough has been done to establish such a school of landscape, as cannot be found on the rest of the globe.'

Much of the status of the landscape garden was to do with politics. The conceptual underpinning for the 'natural' look was seen to be freedom or liberty, and it was firmly based on property – land, and plenty of it, allowing the sometimes vast acreages of the landscape garden or park to thrive. The majority of such large estates were held by Whig grandees. As we have seen, politics in this connection had two dimensions, party and international.

It has become a commonplace that the landscape garden has come to be regarded as the single greatest contribution of Britain to the fine arts. From Thomas Gray asserting in 1763 that laying out gardens was England's one original taste or talent, this claim has been sustained through to Nikolaus Pevsner in the 1940s and more recent writers.

In this chapter the principal theorists and writers will be surveyed so as to bring out their importance relative to each other and to the time. Their significance, and what was achieved on the ground, either by them directly or as a result of their influence or inspiration, will be considered in later chapters as appropriate.

Right through the century authors would express an opinion on what a garden ought to be, ranging from satire (Pope) to the serious analytical text of Whately. At all times either poetry or prose might be employed, culminating in the two-pronged polemics on the Picturesque in 1794, one a poem (*The Landscape*) and the other an extended treatise (*An Essay on the Picturesque*). The form of the essay flourished in such periodicals as *The Guardian* or *The Spectator*, with much of the material directed either to moral improvement or to inculcating taste.

The great era of writing on the 'natural' garden started *c* 1710. The Whig Joseph Addison is famed as an essayist, in particular for his creation of Sir Roger de Coverly, a country squire through whom a range of topics relating to taste and fashion could be discussed. In *The Spectator* for 25 June 1712 he argued for the inclusion of natural scenery in a view – 'we take Delight in a Prospect which is well laid out, and diversified with Fields and Meadows; Woods and Rivers' – and that by adding a little art to what nature had provided, 'a Man might make a pretty Landskip of his own Possessions'. Later that year another essay painted a picture of a jumble of artifice and natural growth in a garden, with planted orchards mingling with woodland trees, although no such garden yet existed in reality. Addison discussed in his essays the pleasures of the imagination, where the reader was encouraged to use features seen during a walk or ride to stimulate the imagination and thereby enhance the experience, a way of responding to a garden which reverberated through the century.

Alexander Pope was small in stature (4' 6") but a giant of literature and unquestionably the greatest poet of the century. In prose he satirised extremes of topiary (*The Guardian*, 1713), with a catalogue of such items to be disposed of as St George, cut in box, with his arm not fully grown, 'but will be in a Condition to stick the Dragon by next *April*'. Later, in his *Epistle to Lord Burlington* [of Chiswick], 1731, he lambasts symmetry in gardens, where 'Grove nods at Grove, each Ally has a brother, / And half the Platform just reflects the other'. But he also puts forward positive principles − 'In all, let *Nature* never be forgot' and 'Consult the *Genius* of the *Place* in all' − both of which underpin the development of the landscape garden.

Some of Pope's most striking *dicta* on gardens were remarks caught and recorded by his friend Joseph Spence, including 'all the beauties of gardening might be comprehended in one word, variety' and 'All gardening is landscape painting'. Spence, Professor of Poetry at Oxford and vicar at Byfleet in Surrey, also recorded several observations by Philip Southcote of Woburn Farm close by. Southcote revealed his thoughts particularly on using the techniques of a painter, such as perspective, to produce a result that was comparable to what an artist would achieve, for example, 'In gardening the *principal view* is to be observed as the *principal object* is in a picture.'

The 3rd Earl of Shaftesbury has already been quoted for his passionate belief in nature. However, although he is seen as a leading philosopher of the time, his influence on gardens, if any, never seems to have been recognised by other writers. Ironically his own garden at Wimborne St Giles, Dorset, had to wait for his son, the 4th Earl, until it could be landscaped in the pictorial style.

These early years also saw the rise of the topographical poem, looking at the associations and responses evoked by natural scenery. Pope's youthful pastoral, *Windsor Forest* (1713) was followed in 1726 by John Dyer's *Grongar Hill*, in the Towy Valley, South Wales, where he moralises on the scene. The next year Sir John Clerk of Penicuick, near Edinburgh, penned *The Country Seat*, which demonstrates that from an early date spectacular scenery was brought into the view of Scottish country estates.

With regard to gardens, two pioneers were Stephen Switzer and Batty Langley. Switzer was both theorist and practical gardener. He designed gardens, was a nurseryman and seedsman, and wrote manuals on gardening. His *The Nobleman, Gentleman, and Gardener's Recreation* of 1715 was expanded into his most famous work, *Ichnographia Rustica* (three vols, 1718, revised 1742), and the three areas he particularly made his mark in were extensive or rural gardening (*see* Chapter 4), the *ferme ornée* (Chapter 11) and water management and engineering (*A General System of Hydrostaticks and Hydraulicks*, 1734). He was an industrious author who also wrote the manuals *The Practical Fruit Gardener* (1724) and *The Practical Kitchen Gardener* (1727) and edited the collection of essays forming *The Practical Husbandman and Gardener* in 1733.

Batty Langley, Twickenham nurseryman and Freemason, published *New Principles of Gardening* in 1728, which showed how much he was in the Switzer mould and adopted his ideas (*see* Chapter 5). His other practical works at the time were *A Sure Method of Improving Estates by Plantations* (also 1728) and *Pomona,* or the Fruit Garden Illustrated (1729). A survey of English houses and gardens was planned but never completed. In later years he turned to architecture, producing *Ancient Masonry* (1736) and the pattern book *Ancient Architecture Restored and Improved* (1741–42), the two parts of which were amalgamated in 1747. His understanding of Gothic was, however, dismissed by Thomas Gray (among others), who complained that he had 'published a book of bad Designs'.

Robert Castell, under the patronage of Lord Burlington, published a strange and somewhat fanciful account of Pliny the Younger's description of his estates at Tusculum and Laurentum under the title of *The Villas of the Ancients Illustrated* (1728). On one hand it was a piece of propaganda, purporting to show the resemblance between Pliny's villas and Chiswick (Fig 3.1), and on the other it shows how much the culture of the period was still under the sway of classical times.

Fig 3.1
Robert Castell's plan of Pliny's garden at Tusculum, from *The Villas of the Ancients Illustrated*, 1728.
[Private collection]

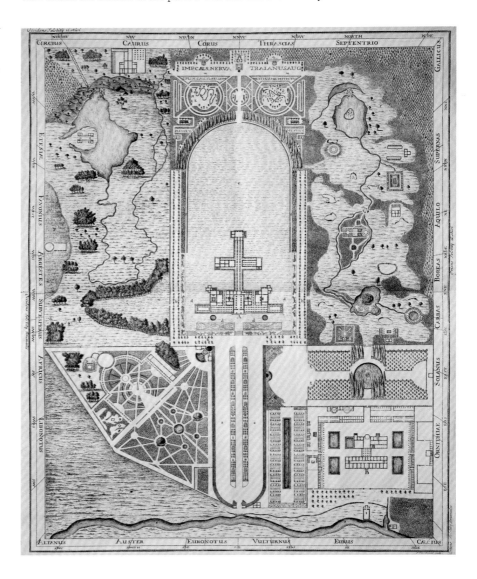

Despite adherence to a basic geometry of design near the house, there are signs of the importance of views of the countryside outside and the *imitatio ruris*.

If Pope was the leading poet of his time, James Thomson wrote the best-selling poem of the century, *The Seasons* (1726–30). The poem, both describing and reflecting on the scenes featured, was expanded in 1744 to include a rhapsodical account of Hagley, commenting especially on its capacity to release the imagination. Thomson also wrote *Liberty*, with particular reference to Stowe embodying that quality in the post-1733 Whig opposition phase.

A phenomenon of the 1740s was the so-called 'Graveyard School' of poetry. Robert Blair's *The Grave* (1743) was contemporary with Edward Young's prolonged *Night Thoughts* (1742–45), perhaps more popular on the Continent than in Britain. Most famous of all was Thomas Gray's *Elegy in a Country Churchyard* (in revised form, 1751). While not directly about gardens these poems reflected melancholy and a prescient taste for Gothic horror that would be perceived as feeding into gardens and into the Picturesque. Gray was a keen traveller and botanist, and William Gilpin reckoned he had the greatest powers of observation of nature of any man. Gray's later poem *The Bard* is redolent of the Wild Picturesque, suffused with a defiant nationalism.

Pope died in 1744, the same year that saw the birth of two significant works. One was *The Enthusiast* by Joseph Warton, a young man's rebellion against the established baroque garden in favour of wild nature, condemning Versailles and even questioning Kent's supposedly 'natural' designs. The other was the prose *Pleasures of the Imagination* by Dr Mark Akenside. Once more the importance of the imagination surfaces, this time particularly in response to terrifying and sublime scenery, thereby anticipating Edmund Burke.

William Shenstone was one of the shakers and movers of the landscape garden. For his achievements the reader is referred to Chapters 8 and 11. He was a minor poet who enjoyed a modest reputation in his day, although Dr Johnson did not think much of him. There is little in his poetry relating to gardens, although he composed verses for inscriptions at The Leasowes, but his letters contain much that refers to garden-making, plus descriptions of, and comments on, gardens he had visited. The main source for his opinions, however, is his 'Unconnected Thoughts on Gardening', which forms a section in Dodsley's publication of his works after his death. He divided gardens into parterre, kitchen and landscape, with the focus being on 'landskip or picturesque-gardening', by which he meant a garden that forms a number of pictures. The aim of such a garden is to provide the pleasures of the imagination and to produce agreeable sensations: 'It consists in pleasing the imagination by scenes of grandeur, beauty, or variety.'

Contemporary with Shenstone was his close friend and fellow student at Oxford, Richard Graves. He had wide-ranging interests and was a poet, critic, essayist and novelist. His two principal novels, *Columella* and *The Spiritual Quixote*, satirise Shenstone good-humouredly. Both are worth reading for the material on The Leasowes, and *Columella* mentions many landscape garden features. Richard Jago, another close friend, was responsible for the topographical poem *Edge-Hill* (1767), which describes several estates including The Leasowes.

Head and shoulders above everyone else for discoursing (often in highly quotable form) on gardens, as indeed on most aspects of life at the time, was the supreme social commentator Horace Walpole. In addition to his assiduous correspondence (published in 48 volumes), there are references to gardens in his 'Visits to Country Seats', but the central work was his *History of the Modern Taste in Gardening*, written by 1770 but not published until a decade later. In this he adopts a historical approach, with the purpose of demonstrating how vastly superior the landscape style was to the formal aberrations and monstrosities that had preceded it.

In the 1750s a periodical called *The World* came out, edited by Edward Moore. This published essays on various subjects, but notably gardens, for which the authors included Walpole, Francis Coventry and Richard Owen Cambridge. Coventry is best remembered for his contribution to issue 15 (1752), in which he satirised the rococo assemblage of the gardens of a Squire Mushroom, 'which contain every thing in less than two acres of ground. At your first entrance, the eye is saluted with a yellow serpentine river, stagnating through a beautiful valley, which extends near twenty yards in length'. Cambridge, noted wit and christened 'King of Twickenham', wrote a series of pieces which included a denial of Chinese influence on the English garden. At church one Sunday he seemed distracted, and when his wife asked of what he was thinking, he replied, 'Of the next *World*, my dear.'

William Gilpin is sometimes said to be the mainspring of the Picturesque. From quite early on (1748, in a description of a tour round Stowe) he formed the idea of the desirability of landscape (and hence gardens) forming a series of pictures, and defined the Picturesque as 'a term expressive of that peculiar kind of beauty, which is agreeable in a picture'. Through his tours of various parts of the British Isles, which were published after a time lag of a decade or more, he developed his ideas, being drawn more and more to the attractions of wild and mountainous scenery. What distinguished him from the picture-making of Kent and others from a previous generation was his assessment of scenery as if it constituted a picture, to the extent of altering reality to conform to his aesthetic ideals when he came to sketch scenes on his tours.

George Mason published *An Essay on Design in Gardening* anonymously in 1768. It covered the history of gardens before going on to praise the landscape garden, with many examples. In some respects it foreshadowed Walpole's more famous essay, while in his descriptions, although briefer, he anticipates Whately a couple of years later. The book was revised and republished in 1795, this time with the author named, and gave Mason the chance to ruminate on the Picturesque Controversy and also to review recent publications on gardens. This allowed him to attack Whately forcefully, quite possibly through envy, because Whately's book had proved far more successful than his own.

William Chambers, knighted in Sweden but not in England, produced, on the basis of two or three restricted visits to China, *Designs of Chinese Buildings, Furniture, Dresses, Machines, and Utensils* in 1757, which included a section, 'Of the Art of Laying Out Gardens Among the Chinese', a fanciful account that was slanted towards the landscape garden. This was expanded and embellished as *A Dissertation on Oriental Gardening* (1772), which pushed further in the direction of the Picturesque and Sublime while also attacking Brown for tameness and monotony.

The Revd William Mason (no relation to George) was, among other things, garden designer and prolific correspondent. Two poems ensure his immortality in the pantheon of 18th-century garden writing: *An Heroic Epistle* (1773), a satire against Chambers' *Dissertation* that ran to 14 editions in four years, and *The English Garden* (1772–81), a protracted work in four volumes, praising the naturalness of the landscape garden but admitting art and encouraging the creation of 'pictures'.

As well as incurring dislike, the Brown style attracted some ridicule. In his poem on Nuneham Courtenay, Oxfordshire, William Whitehead, comfortably one of the worst poets to have held the office of Poet Laureate, had Dame Nature and Brown argue about who was the more responsible for the beauties of the landscape. Brown seems to have won, but Dame Nature has the last word: 'Each fault they call his, and each excellence mine.' In 1775 Joseph Cradock published *Village Memoirs*, which sends up Brown as 'Mr Layout'. There are also some 'Strictures on Landscape Gardening', in which Cradock voices his own thoughts in the persona of one of his characters. These include a preference for the pictorial and natural garden, an acceptance of formal avenues in the right situation and in general a rejection of Brown:

> No wonder that our taste in England is still to be condemned, since most of our largest gardens are laid out by some general undertaker, who, regardless of the peculiar beauties of one situation, introduces the same objects at the same distance in all.

The standard, classic text was *Observations on Modern Gardening* by Thomas Whately. This work not only analysed the components of a landscape garden, both natural and built, with 19 site descriptions, but endeavoured to inculcate taste, particularly of a picturesque kind, and showed how visitors at the time would respond to gardens. It was Whately who highlighted the change from mental to emotional and imaginative response. The book went through six editions in the 30 years from 1770.

Although mainly a writer on agricultural matters, Arthur Young covered gardens in the publication from 1768 of his several tours around the British Isles plus France. Some of the most evocative descriptions are to be found in his accounts. A contemporary, William Marshall, wrote on agriculture and horticulture, his principal publication being *On Planting and Rural Ornament* (1796; published earlier under a slightly different title), which combined instruction with description of gardens and even incorporated Walpole's history essay in full.

While the most popular authors, such as Whately and Chambers, were translated and enjoyed wide circulation on the Continent, there was occasional traffic the other way, principally Daniel Malthus' *An Essay on Landscape* (1783), which translated the Marquis de Girardin's *De la Composition des Paysages* of six years earlier but which added a lengthy preface of Malthus' own to cover a historical survey of gardens. Meanwhile, John Trusler, an author who lived close to Painshill and evidently absorbed much from it, turned his mind to advice on gardens with *Elements of Modern Gardening* (1784). Unusually he spoke about flower gardens and shrubberies in addition to broader effects. The following year saw two papers that were published by learned societies, Daines Barrington's 'On the Progress of Gardening' in *Archaeologia* and William Falconer's 'Thoughts on the Style and Taste of Gardening among the Ancients' in *Memoirs of the Literary and Philosophical Society of Manchester*, the latter covering a history of gardens that was, along with Malthus, commended by Humphry Repton. These papers indicate the seriousness with which the subject of gardens was taken, and presage garden history as a fitting academic subject two centuries before it became established in British universities.

In the 1790s writing was dominated by the Picturesque. Humphry Repton, who became a practitioner at the age of 36 in 1788, presented his clients with a Red Book (*see* Chapter 15) which contained both handwritten text and watercolour illustrations, but his published works reproduced a certain amount from the Red Books as well as expanding on theory. The four main works were *Sketches and Hints on Landscape Gardening* (1795), *Observations on the Theory and Practice of Landscape Gardening* (1803), *An Enquiry into the Changes of Taste in Landscape Gardening* (1806) and *Fragments on the Theory and Practice of Landscape Gardening* (1816). While showing some sympathy with the Picturesque, Repton took a pragmatic rather than an ideological view and concentrated on pleasing his client, whose comfort and convenience were paramount. The books contain interesting sections on optical and colour theory, and represent comprehensive handbooks on how to devise a landscape garden in the new cultural climate. It was inevitable that he would fall foul of the two extreme proponents of the Picturesque, Price and Knight (*see* Chapter 14).

Those two Herefordshire squires initially constituted a formidable team in proposing that gardens should be composed on the examples and principles of painting, but later fell out with each other, as they did with many others. It was in 1794 that they jointly set out their polemical stalls, Price with *An Essay on the Picturesque* in prose and Knight with *The Landscape* in verse. Both were revised and reissued to take on board the objections and criticisms that had met the original publications. Price made a further attempt to explain his thinking and convey it in more reader-friendly form in *A Dialogue on the Distinct Characters of the Picturesque and the Beautiful* in 1801.

The Picturesque was more or less a spent force by 1810, but that did not stop authors poking fun at it. William Combe presented Gilpin in the title role of *The Tour of Dr Syntax in Search of the Picturesque* (1812), illustrated by Rowlandson, retailing far-fetched adventures in the Lake District. Jane Austen had more muted fun with Repton in *Mansfield Park* (1814) and sent up Gothic horror in *Northanger Abbey*. Thomas Love Peacock mocked both Repton, in the person of Mr Milestone, and the Picturesque itself in *Headlong Hall* (1815).

4 | Extensive, rural or forest gardening

Extensive, rural or forest gardening were important developments that entered the story at an early stage and laid the foundation for what was to come by focusing on woodland, which in itself bore a natural appearance and assumed a crucial role as a major determinant of the look of the garden as a whole. There was also a practical purpose to planting trees or conserving existing woodland – the need to replenish the nation's stock of timber to satisfy the demands of the Navy at times of war. John Evelyn in the later 17th century had urged the planting of timber to this end. Establishing or continuing long-term dynasty at an estate was a further motivation.

Stephen Switzer stands at the centre of this triple concept, the components of which often overlap. He has not always received due credit for what he achieved, partly because his designs were still largely geometrical, but a definitive study published in 2017, *Ichnographia Rustica: Stephen Switzer and the Designed Landscape*, by William Brogden, fittingly raises his profile.

Switzer combined theory with practical instruction on design and agriculture, and urged the combination of the pleasurable with the profitable. His plea for cutting down on expense as well as increasing income from the land would have appealed to many of the less wealthy, but it also pointed the way towards the landscape garden without saying so. At the time of Switzer's early career and indeed of his maturity, gardens were still largely formal, and Switzer's design innovations, such as the military bastion wilderness and extended walk at Grimsthorpe, Lincolnshire (where vestiges survive), remain within a geometrical framework. Nonetheless the purpose was to provide views over the fields and the more natural parts of the estate or even outside it.

Just as Addison had expressed a wish for mixing up the various components of a garden, whether productive or ornamental, so Switzer applauded their juxtaposition: 'And why, is not a level easy Walk of Gravel or Sand shaded over with Trees, and running thro' a Corn Field or Pasture Ground, as pleasing as the Largest Walk in the most magnificent Garden one can think of?' We are on the way to the *ferme ornée* (*see* Chapter 11). And, following Shaftesbury, Switzer queried large-scale earth moving to create formal splendour: 'Again, why should we be at that great Expence of levelling of Hills, or filling up of Dales, when they are the Beauty of Nature? Why should we esteem nothing but large regular Walks, the only Characteristicks of a noble Seat?'

Switzer declares that a large garden should be viewed from a circuit on horseback or by horse-drawn chaise. This concept is enormously important to the development of the landscape garden, whether leading to Brown's perimeter ridings or the basis of the pictorial garden, where the great innovation was that it should be walkable as well.

He also argues for the correct choice and placement of sculpture: thus, the right place for a statue of Flora is a flower garden, while Neptune should rise from a pool. This indicates he is still thinking largely in terms of the formal (or mainly formal) garden, because Graeco-Roman sculpture is itself a sign of the Augustan Age and the classically educated owner or visitor. With regard to the scale of a garden, Switzer disapproves of vast tracts of lawn, but instead promotes woodland (hence 'forest gardening'), provided it occurs in the right places and does not spoil the view. The finest example of forest gardening is Cirencester Park, where existing woods were augmented and merged around the astonishing central axis of the six-mile ride to Sapperton village. Wray Wood, at Castle Howard, a little way from the house and at the top of the slope, had been designed by George London; Switzer probably had input into its revision, although Nicholas Hawksmoor was primarily responsible for making it the cultural centrepiece of the garden. Castle Howard is, in any case, an early example of what John Harris termed a 'templescape', a landscape dotted strategically with features on open ground (the Mausoleum (Fig 4.1), Pyramid and Temple of the Four Winds) or within a grove (the Four Faces). Naturalness permeated the wider design, although not Switzer's work, as far as is known.

Fig 4.1
Mausoleum at Castle Howard.
Engraving by Hawksworth after
Thomson for *The Beauties of
England and Wales*, 1812.

For an example of 'rural gardening', Switzer chose Dyrham Park, Gloucestershire, a formal garden transformed into a landscape park late in the century. Although formal, emphasis is on the natural beauties of the scene, with 'rural' implying the countryside.

'Extensive gardening', by the choice of adjective, clearly implies a layout on a grand scale, looking ever outwards. Gardens of initially baroque appearance (as illustrated in Kip and Knyff) could be adapted, and even where Switzer was not personally involved, the opportunities to landscape were there in embryo. Sometimes it would take time to re-cast a large estate, such as Badminton, where the basic structure survived, although by mid-century there were more decorative and modern touches. Switzer's own plans as set out in *Ichnographia Rustica* show how a whole estate could be designed, with irregularity and asymmetry prominent, although amid a welter of straight lines, axes and tightly controlled compartments (Fig 4.2).

Switzer's management of water was a speciality. A forerunner of Brown in this respect, he devised and described projects for cascades, raising water and so on, and from his illustrations we can see elaborate schemes, such as the cascade at Spye Park,

Fig 4.2

Plan of a forest or rural garden, from Stephen Switzer, *Ichnographia Rustica*, II, Plate 33, 1718. [Private collection]

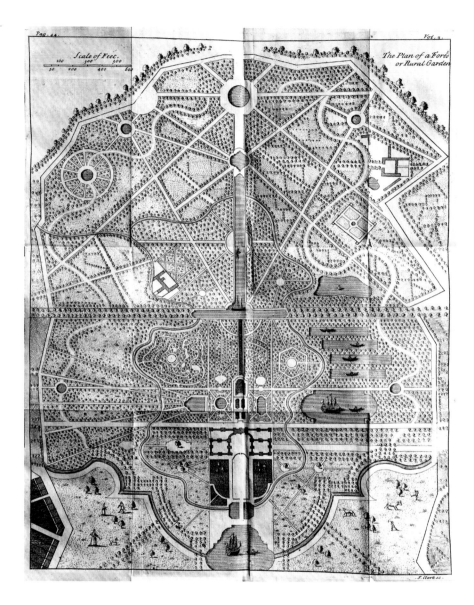

Wiltshire. The problem with such substantial formal structures is that (a) they were expensive to maintain and (b) would in many instances have been superseded by the landscape movement.

Little has survived of Switzer's work, certainly in anything like its original form, but in many ways he opened the door to future developments – and that at a surprisingly early date. By 1712, as Dr Brogden points out, Switzer had loosened up Wray Wood; had been praised for consulting the Genius of the Place at Kensington Gardens; had welcomed fields into the compass of a garden; had planned the first irregular watercourse; had started on improvements to the wider landscape; and had promoted the farm-like way of gardening.

5 | The 'artinatural' garden

Batty Langley was very much a disciple of Switzer, not to say plagiarist. For example, in his most well-known horticultural work, *New Principles of Gardening*, he includes a section on the appropriate placement of classical statuary in a garden, but that repeats Switzer from a decade earlier. By 1775, however, such concerns were totally out of date and subject to mockery in Joseph Cradock's *Village Memoirs*, where a local squire without classical education orders a Mercury with a quiver and Hercules with a trident. However, Langley – in tandem with Switzer – promoted what is sometimes called a transitional style of garden, heavily geometrical still but with variety, freedom from symmetry and scope for rococo intricacy in some of the compartments or 'garden rooms'. When Langley exclaimed, 'Nor is there any Thing more ridiculous and forbidding, than a Garden which is regular', it was symmetry and repetition that he castigated. Instead Langley called for an 'artinatural' appearance, or 'irregular regularity'.

Picking up on Addison, and once again echoing Switzer, Langley proposed the mingling of garden, farm and countryside: 'Little Walks by purling Streams in Meadows, and through Corn-Fields, Thickets, &c. are delightful Entertainments.' He also recommended incorporating views of distant hills in a park. He was keen on architectural features, and published a number of plates in his book that illustrated views of Roman ruins to terminate an allée: 'which *Ruins* may either be *painted upon Canvas*, or actually built in that Manner with *Brick*, and *cover'd with Plaistering* in Imitation of Stone' (Fig 5.1). The latter practice was often adopted in the pictorial garden of a later generation, particularly where the owner could not afford stone (timber could also be painted to resemble stone, as with the Gothic Temple at Painshill). Langley was also early in the field of producing artificial stone, and made a 'grotesque' temple of the material in a garden on the Westminster riverside.

Although the artinatural garden could be created *de novo*, it was a useful means to impose irregularity and some degree of naturalness on an existing site that was firmly based on an axial framework. In such cases the irregularity would be introduced at the side, or in the interstices, of the broad straight walks or avenues, which would remain. It was also a way of preserving the formal lines and features of a treasured layout even in the age of full landscaping. So at Wrest Park, Bedfordshire, the design, centred on a canal leading to Thomas Archer's grand pavilion (together with one attributed to Langley), remained at the heart of the later 18th-century makeover, where Brown encircled it with a sinuous lake and introduced perimeter landscaping (Fig 5.2).

Fig 5.1
Suggestions for the termination of walks, from Batty Langley, *New Principles of Gardening*, Plate XX, 1728. [Private collection]

Fig 5.2
Modern plan of Wrest Park.
[© Historic England Archive,
MP/WRE 0060]

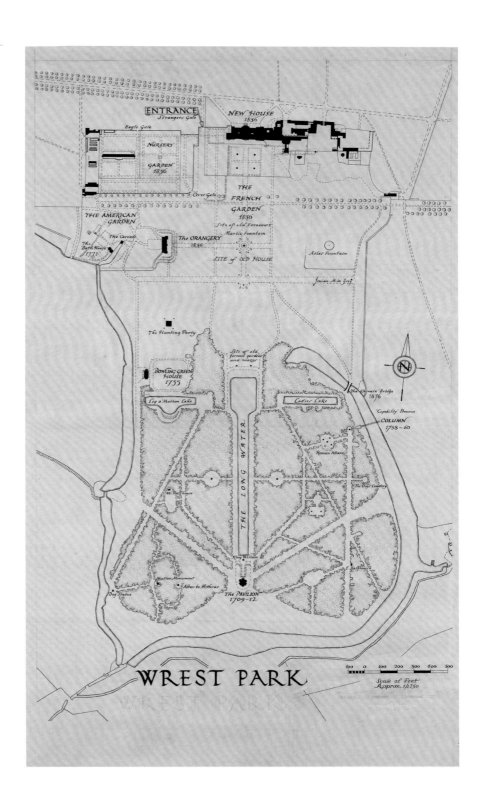

Fig 5.3
Hedgework at Bramham.

Fig 5.4
Moon Ponds at Studley Royal,
drawn and engraved by Anthony
Walker, 1758.

Some gardens, although not created as artinatural, would pass through a coexistence of artificial and natural design, as at Stowe, the grandest of all, before landscaping took the upper hand. In others the formality remained, to give the garden its predominant character, although subsequent landscaping provided balance beyond the formal centre. Two great Yorkshire gardens will illustrate the point: Bramham, near Leeds, the fame of which rests on the early 18th-century French-style waterworks, straight paths and allées and tall clipped hedgework (Fig 5.3), and Studley Royal, near Ripon, where the Moon Ponds are perfect in their cool geometry (Fig 5.4). Both, however, were extensively modified by later landscaping that did not interfere with or spoil the formal parts.

Alexander Pope's small garden at Twickenham could well be described as artinatural. From 1719 until his death in 1744 he laboured to produce as much interest as he could within his five acres. His gardener John Serle's plan of 1745 showed a main central axis with some degree of symmetry but also with independent and irregular features off to the sides. Walpole said of the garden that Pope had 'twisted and twirled and rhymed and harmonized' it into a compression of variety and scenery, with woodland concealing the boundaries and therefore the limited extent.

There are signs that Kent took his structure of the garden at Carlton House (*see* Chapter 7) from Pope, which suggests that his garden had become a model for design on a small scale. Moreover, the artinatural soon showed itself to be a template for gardens of various sizes. At South Dalton Hall, Yorkshire, a formal canal was

surrounded by woodland with paths wriggling around within. The most famous was Chiswick, where Lord Burlington initially laid out a highly axial garden to complement, stylistically, his quasi-Palladian villa. The plan was based on straight walks, a canal, and a series of three 'goose-foot' patterns. Yet there were sinuous paths in the woodland, an irregular embankment walk and indications of straying from regularity even before Kent came on the scene.

Switzer's designs clearly indicate a measure of the artinatural, particularly with regard to wiggles and lack of symmetry, and likewise do some of Charles Bridgeman's. For all that he is generally classified as a baroque formalist, Bridgeman did produce some quirky irregularities and asymmetrical twirlings in designs such as for Down Hall, Essex, Farley, Berkshire, or Rousham, the drawing of which shows how much Kent depended on his basic structure for his own landscaping.

The grander the garden the more likely it was that formality would linger on, perhaps in modified or restricted form. When Brown was made Royal Gardener in 1764 he refused to landscape Hampton Court, leaving the yew parterre, Long Water and lime avenues as they were; likewise at Blenheim and Wimpole, where lined avenues march away for some distance from the house. At Badminton the most magnificent of avenues radiated from the house across an estate that spanned three counties, and those avenues remained, allowing much scope for landscaping the park and farmland in between. The most famed garden of all, Stowe, retains elements of formality to this day, despite radical landscaping since its early strictly ordered inception.

Several artinatural layouts are recorded in the engraved plans of John Rocque (mainly 1730s and 1740s), giving us a valuable picture of the state of gardens at a time when full-blown naturalistic landscaping was still to come. They also often indicate formal features such as regular shapes of water that were later refashioned into something more natural in appearance, or the formal terrace at Oatlands, Surrey, which was later expanded and softened to create a broad, curved viewing platform (Fig 5.5).

Fig 5.5

Terrace and Broadwater at Oatlands, drawn and engraved by Luke Sullivan, 1759.

6 | Garden iconography

Garden iconography, where some kind of symbolism or programme of associations is present, belongs more to formal gardens than it does to the landscape garden, although it may surface from time to time either in built structures or in plantings (for instance, an emphasis on native rather than imported foreign species, thereby making a nationalistic point). It is most clearly discernible in buildings or in sculpture, particularly where those features have a specific name, such as a Temple of Venus. Garden iconography was at its height in the Italian Renaissance garden, although it had a second flowering in the wonders of Louis XIV's Versailles and in other baroque palaces such as Het Loo, the Netherlands. In Britain many formal gardens did not have coherent emblematic schemes, but a regular layout would facilitate such programmes.

In order to work, iconography has to be understood by an educated visitor. Thus in Britain it was in the Augustan Age that it chiefly flourished, with the implicit acknowledgement of the supremacy of classical literature and culture. The majority of iconography, accordingly, relates to classical subjects, although it may point to local, topical or political applications. For deeper and detailed study of the whole area of iconography in the garden, from narrow to broad, the reader is referred to the *New Arcadian Journal*, under the editorship of Patrick Eyres, which concentrates on the 18th century and in particular on political implications.

Sculpture lent itself particularly well to symbolism, whether singly or as part of a programme. Much classically-based sculpture had a readily identifiable meaning, perhaps via an attribute or accessory, such as the figure at Powis of Fame with her trumpet (Fig 6.1). An elaborate handbook of symbolism, Cesare Ripa's *Iconologia* had been published in Rome in 1593 and had been used widely as a source throughout Europe. It was not, however, translated into English until 1709, when a plethora of lead figures was emerging from the yard of John Van Nost the Elder. Ripa was expanded in George Richardson's *Iconography, or A Collection of Emblematical Figures, Moral and Instructive* of 1773, but by that time emblematic use of sculpture had largely died down, as indeed had sculpture itself in the landscape garden.

There are collections of (especially) lead figures in the formal gardens of Melbourne Hall, Derbyshire, and Studley Royal; also at Castle Howard and Stowe, where over 200 statues that were originally there are now being replaced, sometimes by replicas. Some programmes can be deciphered, most explicitly at Rousham (*see* Chapter 7), where there is not only symbolism but a subtle distinction between the violent/battle images in stone at the upper level and the softer lead inhabitants of the lower levels, representing love and the countryside. Classical figures, however, although they continued to be supplied by the lead yards, gave way to contemporary figures (soldiers, drummer boys, gardeners: Fig 6.2) or brightly painted *commedia dell'arte* characters, as significance yielded to decoration and entertainment.

Built structures were, however, the most powerful means of getting messages across, partly because of their size, most sculpture having to be appreciated close up. Meanings could be conveyed by the form and architectural style of the structure; by its name, if specified; or by inscriptions. Thus at Stowe, the most iconographical of English gardens, with its vast array of buildings in addition to statuary, the Cave

Fig 6.1 (above)
Fame with her trumpet at Powis Castle. [© National Trust Images/ Andrew Butler]

Fig 6.2 (above right)
Gardener in lead, formerly at Burton Agnes.

of Dido called to mind the tryst of Aeneas and Dido in a cave, which fitted in with what has been identified as a group of buildings expressing erotic love. The problem, however, was that no visitor of the time remarked on the iconography of the built structures, and only Horace Walpole and Gilpin mentioned allusive sculpture, both in connection with the headless statue of a figure taken to be the First Minister, Robert Walpole, standing in the ruined Temple of Modern Virtue. Gilpin thought this an elegant piece of satire: Walpole, displeased with this denigration of his father, opined that satire had no place in a garden.

Politics played a large part in the make-up of Stowe, ranging from party to national. Lord Cobham gathered his 'cubs' or 'Boy Patriots' around him to form a Whig opposition from 1733, and this momentous step led to the appropriation of Gothic to express the liberty believed to have been founded in Magna Carta and which was the battle cry of the disaffected Whigs. James Thomson's poem on liberty saw its inception in Ancient Greece, then a move to Renaissance Italy and a resting place at Stowe. Gothic architecture was seen to represent (a) a native form of architecture (it wasn't) and (b) a virtuous age when liberty was enjoyed. So, at Stowe, the Gothic Temple (Fig 6.3), originally named the Temple of Liberty, pointedly embodied Lord Cobham's philosophy, while the sculpted Saxon deities at one time around it emphasised the message and its native origins, Saxon and medieval often being conveniently blurred at the time.

Fig 6.3
Gothic Temple at Stowe.
[© Michael Cousins]

This did not mean that all Gothic was political. From mid-century, thanks partly to the proliferation of pattern books of Gothic buildings by Batty Langley and others, it became increasingly decorative and chosen to give variety to an owner's choice of follies. At Painshill, for example, Charles Hamilton was self-confessedly apolitical, so his Gothic Temple (Fig 6.4) is there to adorn, not for any ulterior motive.

The two outstanding landscapes in South Yorkshire, Wentworth Castle and Wentworth Woodhouse, were opposed both in location and politically. The gardens could be read to reveal the Jacobite positioning of the first and the orthodoxy of the latter from its artefacts. They exhibited a combination of party politics (Whig vs Tory and Jacobites, who often voted together) and nationalist (Protestant England vs

Fig 6.4
Gothic Temple at Painshill.

rebellious Scotland and Catholic France). Nationalism can also be seen at Stowe in the frieze originally on the Palladian bridge but subsequently moved to the Temple of Concord and Victory, where the continents are depicted bringing tribute to Britannia (Fig 6.5).

Inscriptions were the most overt way to evoke associations and induce appropriate thoughts and feelings. They were of two kinds – commemorative and those which sought to enhance understanding of the building and its role or to boost the view by providing apposite descriptive comment. Whately was scathing about the latter: 'those beauties and those effects must be very faint, which stand in need of the assistance'. The greatest of inscription gardens was The Leasowes (*see* Chapter 8), but Stowe and Hagley each contained a substantial number. In the case of The Leasowes, inscriptions were generally carved on wood or even written in ink on paper and stuck on a board inside a covered structure.

Iconography changed during the century and, with the rise of the visual arts and the perceived need to appeal to the emotions, it became more diffuse and general. Ruins would be a good example. Seldom were sham ruins given a name, but their generic effect was seen to be to produce a pleasing melancholy as the visitor ruminated on the passing of time and the destruction it had wrought. They were, moreover, peculiarly consonant with the Picturesque by virtue of their irregularity of form.

Fig 6.5
**Temple of Concord and
Victory at Stowe.**

7 | William Kent and the pictorial garden

William Kent is frequently said to be the instigator of the landscape garden, Walpole describing him as Lady Nature's first husband, the second being Brown. However, as we have already seen, much was going on already by the time Kent came on the scene in the late 1720s; furthermore, he was far from completely natural in his designs, in all of which straight lines and other geometry remain.

Kent was an artist-of-all-trades – painter, interior decorator, garden designer, architect, and designer of boats and even women's dresses. As an artist he was unremarkable, although he was responsible for the paintings in the interior of Lord Burlington's Chiswick villa. His formative influence was the rich culture (classical and Renaissance) of Italy, where he spent nearly a decade, from 1710 to 1719. Italy coloured much of his subsequent work, to the extent that he became known as 'Signior Kent'. He was taken up by Burlington, the leading patron of the day, who shared his love of Italy, and Kent lived in Burlington House in Piccadilly. It was to be expected, therefore, that Kent should be involved in the ongoing developments at Chiswick, both villa and garden. Ironically it was Burlington's strong Palladianism that restricted Kent in the main to a severe, classical/Renaissance regularity in the gardens, including the formal exedra with its antique statues. He had scope only to make the

Fig 7.1

Cascade and lawn at Chiswick. Engraved after John Donowell for *The Modern Universal British Traveller*, 1779.

cascade more rustic and open up the lawn between the villa and the water (Fig 7.1). The straight Bollo Brook had already been kinked, but Kent made it more natural.

Kent's approach to garden design was that of an artist, sketching how some set pieces in the garden might look rather than properly surveying and drawing up plans as a professional would. There are a few payments recorded to him, but usually it was a case of Lord Burlington loaning him out to his friends. In the absence of documentation it is hard to be sure of what Kent actually achieved, particularly as he often worked on an existing site where the structure had already been determined. In more cases than not that predecessor was Bridgeman. Walpole stressed Kent's painterly technique and declared that 'The great principles on which he worked were perspective and light and shade'. Philip Southcote of Woburn Farm believed that 'Mr. Pope and Mr. Kent were the first that practised painting in gardening'. To design landscape in sketch form did not, however, mean that Kent copied, or was influenced by, the 17th-century Roman *campagna* painters such as Claude or Poussin, as David Jacques has pointed out. Kent's drawings reveal much more his debt to actual Italian gardens and scenery, complete with Italianate trees such as the cypress, and also to rusticity, which affected several of his structures.

Much misunderstanding among garden historians has been caused by a letter from Sir Thomas Robinson to the Earl of Carlisle (Castle Howard), dated 23 December 1734, in respect of the town garden of Frederick, Prince of Wales, at Carlton House:

> There is a new taste in gardening just arisen, which has been practised with so great success at the Prince's garden in Town, that a general alteration of some of the most considerable gardens in the kingdom is begun, after Mr. Kent's notion of gardening, viz. to lay them out, and work without level or line. By this means I really think the 12 acres the Prince's garden consists of, is more diversified and of greater variety than anything of that compass I ever saw; and this method of gardening is the more agreeable, as when finished, it has the appearance of beautiful nature, and without being told, one would imagine that art had no part in the finishing.

Fig 7.2

Garden at Carlton House. Drawn and engraved by William Woollett, 1760.

This sounds as if Kent initiated the new natural style, but in fact it presents an unreal picture. For a start, planning and planting at Carlton House commenced only in September 1734, so Robinson could hardly have seen anything on the ground. Most planting was carried out in 1735 and would have taken time to mature. Building works continued for some time after that, including shell work, gravel paths, urns and Kent's pavilion. Further, Robinson says the garden was 12 acres – that is an exaggeration because it was no more than nine. He claims that Kent worked 'without level or line', but that was because he did not need to. The gardens he worked on had already been laid out and flattened by level and line, which is certainly true of Carlton House. The greatest unmasking of Robinson is John Rocque's plan of 1746 (possibly executed in 1737), which shows a broad central axis, predominant symmetry and even the paths in the wilderness as mostly straight. This is corroborated by William Woollett's engraving (Fig 7.2), which shows pool answering pool and treillage answering treillage. How could anyone describe that as not showing any

trace of art? So where did Robinson get his notions from? Very likely Kent had produced a few semi-naturalistic sketches (one survives) in advance, which were seen by Robinson but not implemented in that way.

Where, then, did Kent's genius lie? Set scenes or tableaux were certainly to the fore, and essential to the concept of the circuit. These were mostly small scale, however, usually consisting of a building backed by trees and with a sloping lawn in front, leading Walpole to comment, 'Kent's ideas were but rarely great'. Several of the estates he worked on were smaller than those designed by Brown and others later on. Plantings were another significant element – Kent's mastery of contrasting open lawn with groves was frequently commented on, as was his balance of lighter against darker foliage. These were epitomised at Claremont and Esher Place. Thomas Whately and Walpole were still in fulsome praise of his plantings in 1770. Kent was praised for his management of water too, often converting a formal pool into a lake, as he did with Bridgeman's round pond at Claremont.

The central problem with Kent is that his naturalism does not seem to be all that evident to modern eyes, whereas in the 18th century that is what he was chiefly lauded for. That is partly as a result of changes in the meaning, or freighting, of 'nature', as was discussed earlier, and partly because naturalistic scenes formed only small parts of several of his works, as at Chiswick or Kensington Gardens, where his Queen's Temple formed a set scene, backed by trees and clear in front to the water, but as a proportion of the garden as a whole it was minute. With Kent, the artist overrode the nature idealist, and his purpose was to produce an effective and memorable set piece, whether that was to be achieved by formality (the exedra at Chiswick, Fig 7.3), a naturalistic setting, or a mixture of the two (Venus's Vale at Rousham, Fig 7.4).

Fig 7.3 (below)
Exedra at Chiswick. Engraved by William Woollett after John Donowell, 1753.

Fig 7.4 (below right)
Cascades in Venus's Vale at Rousham. [© Michael Cousins]

Claremont, Surrey, more famed perhaps at the time than today, pinpoints the problem. Kent's planting was extensive, and he erected a number of buildings, but Bridgeman's geometrical layout remained to a large degree stubbornly intact – and, moreover, lent itself to a series of 'pictures', such as the view up to Vanbrugh's Belvedere. For all that he loosened Bridgeman's circular pond, it took Brown in the 1770s to naturalise the shape as we now see it. The situation is illustrated most starkly in Benazech's engraving (Fig 7.5), showing the all-dominant amphitheatre of Bridgeman: an earlier version also showed Kent's formal cascade to the far left.

Fig 7.5
Amphitheatre, lake and 'New House'
temple on island at Claremont.
Drawn and engraved by Peter-Paul
Benazech, 1754.

It was left to Kent's assistant and successor at Claremont, Stephen Wright, to convert the cascade into a naturalistic cave grotto in 1750 and subsequently cover the amphitheatre with trees and shrubs.

Detailed lists survive of the plantings at Carlton House and Claremont. Although the range of species is not large, the sheer numbers are impressive. Over 15,000 trees were ordered for the small Carlton House grounds, including 1,500 elms, 1,400 hornbeams, 1,000 chestnuts and 500 yews. These were often massed together in groves, prompting Whately to rhapsodise on the management of groups and groves, with their links and undulations, at both Claremont and Esher Place.

It was at Stowe that Kent secured lasting fame (and credit for more than he actually achieved, because his was the only landscape designer's name commonly attached to it until at least the end of the century). The structure of the estate was Bridgeman's; later naturalising was by Brown; and Kent, although he contributed a number of buildings, concentrated his design efforts in the area known as the Elysian Fields. As Southcote put it, ''tis the Elysian Fields that is the painting part of his [Lord Cobham's] gardens'. In other areas, Kent's buildings, ranging from rustic to classical (Figs 7.6 and 7.7), were situated along, and pointed up, the earlier geometrical framework.

Not infrequently, Kent's buildings were infused with iconography, much of it political. It is likely that such programmes were usually devised by others, for instance Queen Caroline in the case of the two iconic buildings in Richmond Gardens, the Hermitage and Merlin's Cave. At Richmond the sense of circuit was marked, as described in the anonymous *A Description of the Royal Gardens at Richmond in Surry* (probably c 1740), which begins with a numbered plan that shows how the features relate to each other. The description reveals that there was a set walk: ''Tis usual to conduct the Company to THE DAIRY ... Passing by the

Fig 7.6 (above)
Hermitage at Stowe.
[© Michael Cousins]

Fig 7.7 (above right)
Temple of Venus at Stowe. Drawn
and engraved by Thomas Medland
for *Stowe: A Description of the
House and Gardens*, 1797.

side of a Canal, and through a Grove of young Trees'. Based on Bridgeman's layout, the plan of the gardens as Kent left them is semi-formal, but there are views of fields and a general feeling of loosening up. There were several buildings on the circuit, most, although not all, by Kent. The two named above were the most well known and discussed. Sadly there is no trace of Kent's work now.

Among other works, Esher Place should be mentioned because although it has all but disappeared under a smart housing development of the 1930s, at the time Walpole thought that Kent was 'Kentissime' there, creating a garden which, while to some extent still geometrical, contained a series of buildings, each in its own setting, and constituting a circuit.

For today's visitor, Kent's masterpiece and the opus that shows his talents best is Rousham, between Oxford and Banbury. From 1738 both house and gardens were altered by Kent, the house in crenellated Gothic style. The layout had originally been by Bridgeman, and much of his underlying structure remained, including the straight Lime Walk and the pools in Venus's Vale, although reshaped. Kent's circuit is cleverly composed so as to make the most of a relatively tight area but with views of the countryside beyond the boundary of the Cherwell. Apart from the Gothic Seat (mirroring the crenellations of the house) at the top, all is classical within but traditional English outside, including Gothic ornamentation added to the mill across the river and a distant eye-catcher arch in a field.

There are all manner of elements contributing energy and variety to Rousham. One is Italian influence – Kent's sketch for Venus's Vale, with its twin rustic cascades, is thought to have been inspired by the garden behind the theatre at Villa Aldobrandini. Then there are the plantings, with underplanting of colourful shrubs among the trees in the woods as described by John Macclary, gardener at the time. The top level is militaristic, as befitted the owner, the retired General Dormer, with a statue of Minerva in her helmet as Goddess of Battle, complemented by the Lion

Fig 7.8
Gothic Seat at Rousham.

Fig 7.9
Temple at Euston Hall.
[© Michael Cousins]

attacking a Horse and the Dying Gladiator. In the garden below, all is rural, fecund and pleasurable – Faun, Pan, Venus, Bacchus, Ceres. The difference is marked, as mentioned before, by the upper statues being of stone and the lower of lead. At the junction are two terms signifying the crossover, Hercules and Pan. Venus's Vale is also theatrical – the statues are the players, looking outwards on their stage. The statuary in niches around the house, including Apollo, Venus, the Dancing Faun, Ceres and a Bacchanal, prefigures whom we are going to meet in the gardens. There is a touch of the *ferme ornée*, with the paddock or pasture cut off by a ha-ha and the Gothic Seat concealing the fact that at the rear it serves as a shelter for the cattle (Fig 7.8). Much of the garden is constructed in triangles: the group of Mercury (as link), Bacchus and Ceres in the amphitheatre; Venus, Pan and Faun in Venus's Vale; Flora and Plenty form a trio with the pediment, itself a triangle, on the Palladian door; Hercules, Pan and the Dying Gladiator; and Venus and her two *amorini* on swans, also in Venus's Vale. Among signs of the 'new' gardening the rill bears a serpentine form, leading to the cold bath.

In the 1740s Kent seems to have expanded his outlook in a more natural idiom. Two examples are Euston Hall, Suffolk (Fig 7.9), and Holkham, Norfolk, where, although he had started devising features several years before, there is a definite open landscape feel. The most extreme case was Worcester Lodge at Badminton, an eye-catcher nearly two miles from the house.

With Kent, then, there is a sense of pushing towards the natural, particularly in plantings and in rusticity of ornament, but his great contribution was the unfurling of the concept of the pictorial garden.

8 | The poetic or literary garden

The garden with literary allusion or reference was a limited genre, and belongs more to the first half of the century, the Augustan Age, reflecting the tendency to a cerebral response to gardens. It would work by means of a specific name of a building or other monument or through inscriptions. A theme, mood or even a whole iconographic programme could accordingly be established. If the inscription was taken from a particular author, there would be the added associations evoked by the name of that author.

The principal poets to be quoted or whose stories would be enlisted were classical, Virgil above all. At home the trio of poets from the past who had established themselves as the monarchs of English poetry were Milton, Spenser and Chaucer. Milton and Spenser were commemorated in various ways, and both pervaded the garden to a degree beyond mere quotation, while Chaucer seems to have been referenced only at Nuneham Courtenay.

In Milton's case, it was often thought (for example by Walpole) that he had anticipated the landscape garden in his description of the Garden of Eden in *Paradise Lost* (1670), which appears to be natural in several respects. More implicit was the notion that the landscape garden was an attempt to recreate the Garden of Eden, and writers at the time would make comparisons when discussing particular sites. Their idea of the paradise garden would be taken largely from Milton although authors from the Bible onwards had described it. Mount Edgcumbe contains both specific and allusive reference to Milton: the so-called amphitheatre (Fig 8.1), stretching back from the sea and rising in cliffs with trees tiered on the sides, is said to have been modelled on the 'walls' of Eden as portrayed by Milton, while a temple dedicated to him stands at the foot, near the sea (Fig 8.2). Similarly the specific and general are

Fig 8.1 (below)
Amphitheatre at Mount Edgcumbe.

Fig 8.2 (below right)
Milton's temple at Mount Edgcumbe.

combined at Hagley. The hermitage contains lines from Milton's *Il Penseroso* on the meditative, and hence melancholy, life, while Milton's Seat celebrated the 'splendid and sublime' panorama (Fig 8.3), obtainable from it by lines from *Paradise Lost*. This time the view is infused with, and filtered through, the Miltonic proclamation of the wonder of God's works.

Fig 8.3
View from Milton's Seat at Hagley.
[© Michael Cousins]

Spenser's impact was rather more visual. William Kent drew a number of scenes from *The Faerie Queene* in a new edition of Spenser's epic, with backgrounds resembling a landscape garden. At Stowe the racy and titillating story of Malbecco and Helinore was illustrated not in verse but by Francesco Sleter's murals (described as 'indelicate') in Kent's Temple of Venus (*see* Fig 7.7). This reference to Spenser is specific, but the Temple can be seen in a wider context, as part of a theme of erotic love, among other themes, at Stowe (*see* Chapter 6). Spenser also made his presence felt at The Leasowes.

Fig 8.4
Congreve monkey monument at Stowe.

Contemporary poets and writers were commemorated in gardens. The Restoration comedy playwright Congreve had a suitably satirical memorial at Stowe in the form of a monkey surveying its reflection in a mirror (Fig 8.4), while Pope was remembered both by quotation (the Nymph of the Grot at Stourhead) and actual memorial – an urn at Hagley together with Pope's Seat, which featured at Cirencester Park as well. James Thomson was remembered at Hagley, his Seat looking across to Pope's, while the neighbouring William Shenstone was acknowledged by an urn. In addition a temple to Thomson was raised at Mount Edgcumbe.

A few inscriptions or memorials did not necessarily confer on the garden as a whole the feeling of a literary garden. Mount Edgcumbe, for example, despite its homage to Milton and Thomson, was far more of a sea-focused picturesque landscape of a largely outward-looking type. Stowe and Hagley carried a great number of inscriptions and references to the classics but, again, they were but one of numerous aspects and dimensions that went to make up these many-layered gardens.

The number of gardens that could be characterised as substantially literary is in fact very small. William Mason's flower garden at Nuneham Courtenay in the 1770s (Fig 8.5) was a landscape garden in miniature, with a circuit encompassing buildings, busts and inscriptions, but instead of extensive park scenery it encircled a small undulating lawn studded with irregular flower beds. As it was a flower garden, a bust of Flora stood at the entrance, to be matched at the opposite end by a temple

Fig 8.5
Flower garden at Nuneham
Courtenay. Engraved by William
Watts after Paul Sandby, 1777.

to the same deity. There were a grotto and a bower, together with memorials of the philosophers Locke and Rousseau and the poets Abraham Cowley and Matthew Prior. The legendarily severe Roman censor Cato was commemorated, principally for his belief in a primitive, simple agrarian way of life, and for his writings, which included a treatise on agriculture and horticulture. There was also an urn to friendship. Inscriptions included quotations from the Italian epic poet Ariosto (who influenced Spenser), Andrew Marvell, Milton and Chaucer, but the presiding spirit was that of Jean-Jacques Rousseau, who had stayed at Nuneham and was said to have sown seeds of foreign wild flowers in the garden. Rousseau was passionate about botany and claimed that its study would make people forget themselves and think of the Great Author of plants. It was, accordingly, a garden that was both literary and inspiring of virtue in the contemplation of nature.

The most literary of gardens was Shenstone's The Leasowes. Although often classified as a *ferme ornée* (*see* Chapter 11), it was created by a poet, albeit a minor one, and comprised a heavily referenced circuit around a pasture farm (Fig 8.6). There were 39 pause points from which to obtain particular views, sometimes of external scenery, and to contemplate, aided by inscriptions on the benches or flimsy structures that were all that the impecunious owner could afford. It was the inscriptions that determined what Shenstone intended to evoke and how his visitors were expected to respond (it went over the heads of many). Virgil was the principal source (12 inscriptions) and Horace furnished several others, all in Latin. However, English was found on the Gothic structures, including a few verses by Shenstone himself, one of which was deliberately lengthy so as to distract the visitor from what was a not particularly interesting view at that point.

One of Shenstone's poems was purportedly written by Oberon, so referred directly to *A Midsummer Night's Dream*; another was couched in pseudo-Spenserian language, Shenstone having failed to find anything suitable in Spenser's own works. The cumulative effect was to evoke a medieval English world, which was visually supported by the half-dozen Gothic constructions. This balanced the summoning of a classical Golden Age through the Latin quotations. Both betray Shenstone's escapist fantasies and also his reliance on quotation – Whately for one disliked inscriptions and considered that in general they 'please no more than once'. Shenstone, brought up in the Augustan Age and in a milieu of like-minded contemporaries, began his garden in the 1740s but by the time of his death, in 1763, when he was still working on it, the concept of a literary garden was somewhat old-fashioned (Nuneham, thanks to Rousseau, although later, grafted on new ideas about nature). However, Shenstone's 'naturalness' was highly praised, and the views, together with plantings, most of which were indigenous, enabled him to vary the mood and to build a visual and emotional climax in the dark and meditation-inducing Virgil's Grove. The Leasowes was enormously popular and enjoyed a high reputation. It had one copy, by Sir Samuel Hellier at the Woodhouse, near Wolverhampton, which consisted of a three-hectare wood with clearings in which a small circuit connected various glades or clearings containing buildings and trees with inscription boards on them. There was an urn to Shakespeare, together with quotations from English poets including Milton and Gilbert West, but the feeling was not primarily literary. The structures were eclectic, including a hermitage, grotto, seats, a root house and a 'Druid's Temple' (a mini-Stonehenge), but music eclipsed literature in the shape of a substantial music room built first, featuring an organ, and a temple dedicated to Handel.

The poetic or literary garden flourished more on the Continent, in some cases owing an evident debt to The Leasowes. The Marquis de Girardin visited Shenstone's estate in 1763, just after the cessation of hostilities, and on return home created the multidimensional gardens of Ermenonville (today the Parc Rousseau), which paid equal respect to Shenstone and the French *philosophe*, who died there, and which were known as the French Leasowes. English authors such as Edward Young and Laurence Sterne were commemorated in other gardens.

9 | The mid-century circuit garden

O f the many forms assumed by the landscape garden, the pictorial circuit garden was the most striking, most visited and reported on, and the type most favoured by those who designed gardens in Europe in the late 18th century. We have seen how Kent pioneered the concept – by mid-century it had become refined and sophisticated in a much more naturalistic setting. It was often the province of the owner/amateur, someone who had creative and individual vision and had no need to call in the services of a pragmatic consultant. And a circuit made the garden independent of the house.

The circuit proved a flexible and therefore a popular medium. It could be firmly delineated by a path, or by a mixture of open ground and paths, and would link the important features of the garden. Sometimes, as at Hagley or West Wycombe, there is a sense of circuit rather than something tangible: in the case of Hagley, no simple circuit can be made to fit, and there is inevitably a certain amount of retracing one's steps. In many instances the circuit is confirmed by visitors' descriptions at the time (for example, several speak of going around Painshill by the same route). A circuit, perhaps psychologically, tends to operate clockwise, although the ultimate circuit garden, The Leasowes, took the opposite direction.

A definite and intended circuit had the great advantage of ensuring that the visitor saw everything the owner deemed of interest, even though that could be regarded as manipulative. It imposed a structure on an otherwise natural-looking landscape, and in addition to linking features within the grounds it could provide optimum vantage points from which to obtain views of distant scenery. A classic example would be the Double View at Piercefield, a seat around an oak tree that afforded spectacular views in opposite directions. A circuit, as opposed to a drive, was to be walked, although in large estates with an extensive circuit horseback or horse-drawn modes were acceptable. The long circuit at Painshill, for instance, could be followed by hiring chaises from a local inn, although most visitors would choose to walk.

There could be more than one circuit, to allow for easy or arduous exercise, as at Mount Edgcumbe, while the later 'sublime' landscape at Hafod had a gentlemen's walk which was longer and rougher than the ladies' walk, thus presenting a choice of scenery. Significantly, at Hafod there was a dearth of built structures and therefore no compulsion to link them. Having a set circuit could pose problems if a subsequent feature appeared that did not fit into the established scheme: the Ruined Abbey at Painshill, put up at the very end of Charles Hamilton's tenure, requires a detour to see it either close up or from across the lake (Fig 9.1).

Thomas Whately believed that a walk around a field could constitute a garden, and this happened on a grand scale at Kew, one of the most visited of gardens. The perimeter walk was highly ornate, populated by a number of buildings designed chiefly by William Chambers, and looked across two vast lawns that were actually cattle pasture (they appear flat and dull in contemporary prints). The lake, now considerably reduced, was a central feature which broke the dullness up and added further ornament of its own, including a bridge, the House of Confucius and a pleasure boat in the form of a swan. The belt walk varied from a classical enfilade

Fig 9.1
Ruined abbey across
the lake at Painshill.

Fig 9.2
Orangery at Kew.

to the east, parallel to Kew Road; a wilderness to the south that led to the exotic trio of Alhambra, Pagoda and Mosque; a small Gothic Cathedral in wood, set back from the path among trees; and a miscellany of other buildings, including the classical Orangery (Fig 9.2).

A circuit did not have to be extensive. A miniature version consisted of a path around the flower garden at Nuneham Courtenay (*see* Fig 8.4; *see* Chapter 8), leading from a bust of Flora at the entrance via various inscriptions and past a bower, grotto and the Temple of Flora. The central lawn was studded with irregular kidney-shaped beds. Slightly larger was the belt walk at Walpole's Strawberry Hill, taking in the 'chapel in the woods' and a shell seat.

Fig 9.3 (below)
Grotto at Hawkstone
(early 20th-century postcard).
[Courtesy Michael Cousins]

Fig 9.4 (bottom)
Hermitage at Painshill.

The circuit was most evident to visitors where there was a guidebook. The earliest was produced at Stowe (1744), with emphasis on the built structures rather than the landscape. This gave a sense of the relationship of one building to the next and contributed to a sophisticated plan. Groups of buildings have been taken to express various themes such as erotic love, friendship, the arts, liberty and patriotism. At Hawkstone, Shropshire, the guidebook (from 1776) took in the follies and the inscriptions (often of a moral kind), but also rhapsodised about the wild and sublime elements, because they constituted the main attraction of the place, emphasising the emotional reaction of the visitor (Fig 9.3).

Even if there was no guidebook as such, there were plenty of descriptions by visitors, both published and unpublished, and it is often possible to determine the route from these. However, descriptions do vary, and sometimes a different sequence is followed, at the whim of the author. Consequently circuits are not 100 per cent applicable.

A circuit was capable of containing a good deal of subtlety and even theatricality. At Painshill the path moves away from a simple lakeside walk to climb uphill towards the Hermitage (Fig 9.4) and Gothic Tower, well away from the water. In the first, surprise view of the park from the Gothic Temple an array of distant buildings met the gaze, each one of a different architectural style (Gothic Tower, rustic hermitage, classical Temple of Bacchus, Turkish Tent, cave grotto and formal bridge). The visitor would be enticed to go and inspect them at close quarters, but the circuit ensured that they could only be reached by an indirect route, thus conforming to Shenstone's dictum that a building should never be approached in the same direction as the eye has taken: 'Lose the object, and draw nigh, obliquely.'

At Stourhead a lakeside circuit takes on further dimensions as one path turns up steeply to the Temple of Apollo (Fig 9.5), while another leads up and away to the convent in the woods. The triangular Alfred's Tower (Fig 9.6) is also set away, somewhat awkwardly, from the ring of follies. The fact that there is a basic circuit, however, has led to a number of attempts to ascribe an iconographical programme to the gardens. These include an interpretation of the circuit as representing the journey of Aeneas in Virgil's *Aeneid*, Book VI.

Fig 9.5 (right)
Temple of Apollo at Stourhead.

Fig 9.6 (far right)
Alfred's Tower at Stourhead.

Hestercombe, Somerset, embodies a remarkable story of a complete landscape garden rescued from oblivion. A circuit has now been reinstated, embracing not only a number of disparate buildings but focal features such as the high cascade and also distant views across Taunton Vale. Some of the buildings are idiosyncratic, such as the Mausoleum (Fig 9.7), never intended as such, although it bears some resemblance to the 'tomb' at Park Place, Henley. In contrast, the circuit at Hardwick Park, County Durham, is virtually all inward-looking as one progresses along the path, to encounter some distinctly quirky follies attributed to James Paine (Fig 9.8).

A circuit might form only part of a larger garden yet still represent a substantial walk. Robert Adam designed a discrete area of pleasure ground at Kedleston, Derbyshire, where the Long Walk wound around a large pasture field through plantings of fragrant and flowering shrubs and trees.

Fig 9.7 (right)
Mausoleum at Hestercombe.

Fig 9.8 (far right)
Ruined tower at Hardwick Park.

Fig 9.9
Dunstall Castle at Croome Court.

There were also outer circuits, a ring of buildings that individually might be out of sight of the house, as at Croome Court, Worcestershire, where Brown's early commission received subsequent architectural additions in the distance, including Adam's ruined Dunstall Castle (Fig 9.9), the Owl's Nest, Pirton Tower, Broadway Tower, Baughton Tower and James Wyatt's Panorama Tower, a very late extra. At Wentworth Woodhouse the outer perimeter is some miles from the mansion, encompassing such unusual structures as Flitcroft's triangular Hoober Stand, Hoyland Law Stand, John Carr's Lady's Folly, Keppel's Column, the Needle's Eye arch (Fig 9.10) and Carr's three-storeyed Rockingham Monument, sometimes referred to as the Mausoleum (Fig 9.11).

Fig 9.10 (below)
Needle's Eye at
Wentworth Woodhouse.

Fig 9.11 (below right)
Rockingham Monument at
Wentworth Woodhouse.

There were several other pictorial gardens of the time where the circuit, if it existed, is indeterminate and visitors needed to devise their own way of seeing all the features of interest. Halswell, Somerset, has a motley selection of follies, ranging from the classical Temple of Harmony and a rotunda known as Mrs Busby's Temple to a mysterious grotto bridge and the rococo Robin Hood's Hut, with its ogee curves. Enville, Staffordshire, had a Chinese temple, rococo boathouse, grotto, Doric portico, fanciful Gothic summerhouse, chapel, a Gothic gateway eye-catcher (Fig 9.12) and a classical rotunda.

From this brief survey of a multitude of varied garden scenes, it will be realised that the key elements were not just the circuit but the wide range of architecture, experiments being possible in the sphere of the garden that would have been too expensive to implement in a house, despite such elaborate *jeux d'esprit* as Strawberry Hill. It was this type of garden that was widely visited from home and abroad and inspired gardens throughout Europe.

Fig 9.12
Gothic gateway at Enville.

10 | Plantings

There is no question that the large-scale introduction of trees and shrubs, particularly from North America during the 18th century, had a radical effect on the appearance of the landscape garden, bringing variety and subtlety to bear in colour, shape and size of new woodland. This was particularly true of owners/ designers who were interested in botany and keen on collecting and growing the latest introductions. In contrast Brown, and some of those who employed him, usually concentrated on native trees in order to produce the desired 'English' effect. Similarly, Shenstone at The Leasowes (*see* Chapters 8 and 11) confined himself to traditional shrubs and flowers as well as trees, to help create the medieval English atmosphere he was aiming at, as did Horace Walpole in the Priory Garden at Strawberry Hill.

With the advent of the landscape garden came changes in the patterns of planting. No longer did the grand formal avenues of identical-looking trees hold sway but a much more varied scene emerged, with groves both open (one could see through them) and closed (with an understorey), clumps, single trees dotted about, thickets and shrubberies. Groves could be of mixed or the same species. Thomas Whately in 1770 defined the differences of these groupings and subdivisions. In themselves the new patterns of planting expressed the freedom and variety of the landscape garden. The century saw not only more sophisticated choice and distribution of trees in the landscape but the development of the shrubbery (a term coined by 1748). Mark Laird has drawn attention to the widespread use of colourful shrubberies, mostly near the house but sometimes well away from it, analysing in particular the 'theatrical' shrubbery, which was tiered with the tallest plants at the back. Several landscape gardens would begin with a shrubbery-lined walk, as at Stowe or Croome.

Since John Tradescant the Younger in the previous century, seeds and plants had been sent over from the newly established colonies in North America, and such species as the tulip tree, black walnut, sweet gum, scarlet oak and the first magnolia in Europe (*Magnolia virginiana*) had arrived by 1700. These were as yet not publicly available, but interest was growing. Mark Catesby lived in Virginia from 1712 to 1719, visited the West Indies and later went on a four-year expedition to Carolina, Florida and the Bahamas. Not only did he send back a great number of plants, including *Magnolia grandiflora*, catalpa (Indian bean tree) and *Wisteria frutescens*, but he also wrote up the natural history of those areas.

The whole business of obtaining and then transporting plants was transformed, and put on a full commercial footing, by the partnership of John Bartram, a Pennsylvania farmer turned botanist, and Peter Collinson, a draper in Mill Hill. From the early 1730s to Collinson's death in 1768, the continuous trade between them produced up to 200 introductions. There was a subscription scheme whereby clients could order five-guinea boxes of about 100 species, mostly of seeds, generally of shrubs or trees. The nucleus of each box tended to remain the same, with new species added as Bartram sent over the yields of his plant-hunting expeditions to the eastern and southern colonies. The recipients were mostly aristocratic owners with large estates to landscape and fill with plantings, but nurserymen and botanic gardens also took advantage.

If North America was the principal source, it was by no means the only one. Peter Collinson had many contacts in Europe and further afield, so was able to obtain the Tree of Heaven (ailanthus) from China and other plants from Persia, Russia, Nuremberg and Siberia. When Charles Hamilton of Painshill was approached by the Abbé Nolin from Paris in 1755, this led the way to accessing material from the French colonies, both in North America (to the west of the British colonies) and Africa, Senegal in particular. Other introductions during the century included the camellia from Japan, the Lombardy poplar from Italy, *Rhododendron ponticum* from Turkey, the buddleia from South America and the tree fern from Australia, after that country was opened up.

The 18th century was the great age of collectors, and plants were no exception to collecting. Motivation, or justification, may have been partly botanical, but the acquisitive impulse was undeniable. The young Lord Petre built up a vast collection of plants and hothouses at his home of Thorndon Hall, Essex, and it took a 16-volume *Hortus Siccus* (herbarium of dried plants) to record the imported species, mostly from North America. After his early death at 29 in 1742, the estimated 219,225 plants in his nurseries were offered for sale. His rival, who outlived him by nearly 20 years, was the 3rd Duke of Argyll, called a treemonger by Walpole. He built up a modest nursery and garden at Whitton, Middlesex, which by 1750 had reached 55 acres. He obtained specimens from North America long before the Bartram–Collinson business, and also accessed material from Spain, Hungary and Russia. He was the first to grow the Lombardy poplar and the paper birch in England.

The 2nd and 3rd Dukes of Richmond at Goodwood, Sussex, had the best collection of hardy exotics in the country, according to Collinson. Much of Lord Petre's collection found its way there. The difference with Petre and Argyll was that Goodwood was a much larger estate into which the plantings fitted as woodland. Other collections in fully fledged landscape gardens could be found at Painshill, Syon, Croome Court, Hagley, Wilton and Bowood. In some cases the groupings of specimen trees would have warranted the later appellation of an arboretum.

Nurseries changed radically with the spate of new introductions and the consequent demand for them. At the beginning of the century the major nursery in England was that at Brompton Park in South Kensington, run by George London and Henry Wise, who became the royal gardeners. Not only were they suppliers but they designed a large number of gardens in the formal, baroque style, and of course provided the vast number of trees required, particularly for the avenues. Later nurseries sprang up both in the metropolis and in the provinces, such as those run by the Telford and Perfect families in Yorkshire, and offered a wide range of species to those who wished to design their own gardens or who had brought a consultant in.

The species grown in the early 18th century were from a restricted range, mostly native, prominently beech, elm, lime and chestnut. Oak might well indicate an ancient planting, either on open ground or in a wood, and sometimes pollarded. Even when Kent came on the scene, the choice was still limited, although his Italianate sketches of garden scenes indicated such Mediterranean trees as the cypress and stone pine, both of which were in fact well established in Britain. He was keenly aware of the impact of plantings and even planted dead trees for effect in Kensington Gardens, although Walpole said he was laughed out of such excess. When exotics arrived, they would usually be grown in conjunction with existing native timber – mature trees would not be felled in the interests of entirely new plantations but incorporated into the overall scene. As Walpole put it, 'The mixture of various greens, the contrast between our forest trees and the northern and West Indian [American] firs and pines, are improvements more recent than Kent, or but little known to him.' By 1763 the

German architect F W von Erdmannsdorff, on a visit to England, was able to comment that the large number of foreign trees gave a landscape a wonderful variety of colour.

Botanic gardens tended to be regular in design, mainly for ease of study and analysis. They were generally areas within a landscape garden, unless they had developed in a purpose-built small site such as the Chelsea Physic Garden or Oxford Botanic Garden. In the case of Kew, however, a modest beginning grew enormously, taking over a large proportion of the grounds without destroying the overall sense of a landscape.

Similarly, flower gardens were usually small, specialised compartments, often walled or fenced, within a larger estate. As to design, they could vary from formal and regular, as with William Chambers' layout at Kew (Fig 10.1), to the more naturalistic creation of William Mason at Nuneham Courtenay (*see* Fig 8.4).

Fig 10.1

Aviary and flower garden at Kew. Engraving by Charles Grignion after Thomas Sandby, 1763.

Planting continued to be officially encouraged, and the Society of Arts awarded medals to those who planted in large numbers (up to millions of trees). It had a high priority, as shown by the government request for all the coastal plantings at Mount Edgcumbe to be felled in 1779 so as to allow a clear view of a possible invasion by the French and Spanish: this sacrifice was recognised as substantial, and the owner was created Viscount as compensation.

William Gilpin, for one, took the aesthetics of planting seriously, particularly in relation to the Picturesque. He favoured trees that bore signs of individuality, such as an irregular, withered top, and preferred an odd number for groups, usually three (Fig 10.2).

While Brown often cultivated the 'English' look by concentrating on native species, those who were more botanically adventurous were enabled to create a wide spectrum of effect. As Walpole wrote:

The introduction of foreign trees and plants, which we owe principally to Archibald duke of Argyle, contributed essentially to the richness of colouring so peculiar to our modern landscape...The weeping-willow and every florid shrub, each tree of delicate or bold leaf, are new tints in the composition of our gardens.

Fig 10.2
Group of three trees, from
Gilpin's Forest Scenery, 1883.

'GILPIN'S FOREST SCENERY.'

239

Three ill-shaped trees, formed into a good group.
[*Page* 241.

11 | The *ferme ornée*

We have seen that Switzer, to all intents and purposes, established the concept of the *ferme ornée*, even though aspects of it can be traced back to Palladian Italy and further back to Roman times. The term itself means 'ornamented farm', that is, a farm that has had decoration added to it. The farm is therefore at the centre of the concept, and this is reflected in the names of two of the most important examples, Dawley Farm and Woburn Farm. Even if there were attempts at the time to define the term (Whately being the most notable example), subsequent applications of it have been much looser, covering many estates where there were agricultural areas, especially pasture, within the estate and which were made to feature prominently in the view as one went around. It thus bears a close relation to the circuit walk.

The principal instances recognised at the time were pre-existing farms which were gradually developed in the form of an elaborate circuit around the farm, passing alongside the fields. Later the fields themselves might be adorned with specimen trees. This would be especially true of parkland used as pasture, where the young trees had to be protected against browsing animals (Ashburnham, Fig 11.1). In hindsight many more estates have been labelled *fermes ornées* where there was a significant farm element in the view, as at Stowe, with its (grazing) Hawkwell Field and horse paddock, or Wotton. The definition has become so elastic that discrete areas within a layout have individually been so described, and on the Continent even single ornamented farm buildings have been given the appellation.

Fig 11.1
Ashburnham. Engraving by William Watts after Lord Duncannon, 1784.

Two early examples were Riskings (or Riskins/Richings), Buckinghamshire, and Dawley, Middlesex, both Tory projects in the age of Whig ascendancy. It is quite clear that both were political statements, inveighing against what was seen as the extravagance and waste embodied in some grand Whig properties. Riskings, four miles from Dawley, was the second seat of Lord Bathurst of Cirencester Park, while Dawley was acquired by Henry St John, first Viscount Bolingbroke, on his return from exile in France. The existing Dawley Manor was immediately rechristened Dawley Farm, to indicate its priority as a useful and productive estate: as Pope expressed it, ''Tis use alone that sanctifies expense.' Four hundred acres of parkland were converted into farmland, while paintings in the hall of the house depicted rakes, scythes and harrows combined with scenes of agricultural activity.

Thomas Whately, taking a purist line, regarded Woburn Farm (between Weybridge and Chertsey, Surrey, now St George's School) as the supreme – and perhaps the only real – example of the genre. This was because it was seen as a full integration of farm and garden (Fig 11.2). Stemming from a walk linking the fields for practical purposes, the gardens eventually reached 125 acres, divided into 35 acres of pleasure ground and the rest farmland, two-thirds pasture and one-third arable. The broad walk led through all parts, and varied considerably. Sometimes of gravel, sometimes of sand, it wound its way through clumps of evergreens, shrubs and beds of flowers, tiered borders or a thick hedgerow with scented and flowering creepers. There were a few buildings, such as an octagonal summer house and a ruined chapel (Southcote was a Catholic), and the farm animals, along with their sounds and smells, came very close.

Fig 11.2
Woburn Farm. [After Luke Sullivan, *England Display'd*, 1769]

The other great example of a *ferme ornée* has always been taken to be The Leasowes (*see* Fig 8.5), yet Whately did not judge it to be so. He called it a 'pastoral' farm, the word embracing both pasture and literary pastoral. Whately detected at The Leasowes a simplicity absent from Woburn Farm and summed it up thus: 'It is literally a grazing farm lying round the house; and a walk, as unaffected and as unadorned as a common field path, is conducted through the several inclosures.' Although the pasture could be seen from time to time, it was often excluded from sight, and the external views, stretching across to Wales, were more spectacular. It may be more rewarding to consider The Leasowes as a literary garden, as discussed in Chapter 8.

In the second half of the century the concept of the *ferme ornée* declined, to be partly replaced by the model farm, where the latest agricultural methods were employed and farm buildings were designed by leading architects such as Samuel Wyatt. Such buildings therefore had architectural and aesthetic appeal. Model farms were developed at Windsor Great Park, Holkham in Norfolk, and Shugborough (Fig 11.3), among others.

It appears that, although the ideology of yoking the productive with the pleasurable continued to hold validity, in practice it did not seem to work well. Whately summed up the drawbacks:

> Though a farm and a garden agree in many particulars connected with extent, yet in *style* they are the two extremes. Both indeed are subjects of cultivation; but cultivation in the one is *husbandry*, and in the other *decoration*: the former is appropriated to *profit*, the latter to *pleasure*: fields profusely ornamented do not retain the appearance of a farm; and an apparent attention to produce, obliterates the idea of a garden.

This was echoed over 30 years later by Repton:

Fig 11.3
Farm buildings at Shugborough.
[© Crown copyright,
Historic England Archives]

> the country gentleman can only ornament his place by separating the features of farm and park; they are so totally incongruous as not to admit of any union but at the expence either of beauty or profit ... after various efforts to blend the two, without violation of good taste, I am convinced that they are, and must be distinct objects, and ought never to be brought together in the same point of view.

12 | The terrace walk

The terrace walk represents a significant aspect of the landscape garden, if small in number, because the essence was providing an outward view over the countryside, thus fulfilling the concept of 'calling in the country' perfectly. It derived from a straight walk traversing the back of the house, looking over and across a formal sunken parterre. The patterning of a parterre could only be fully appreciated from a raised viewpoint (usually the *piano nobile* of the house). Formal gardens such as Bridgeman's would often have a raised walk or embankment, as at Stowe or Sacombe, Hertfordshire, and again one can see the idea in embryo. Raised walks indeed continued to feature in gardens later on, although not so prominently as those described below.

The terrace walk was amplified and developed so that more distant scenery, outside the boundaries of the garden, could be viewed. In some instances the walk may have been based on an earlier formal one, such as at Oatlands, Surrey, where a straight walk with bulbous circular ends became considerably longer, in a natural curve, although still flat. It was grassed and broken up by one or two trees and seats (*see* Fig 5.5). The views across the Thames Valley were spectacular, causing Robert Dodsley to exclaim in 1761, 'its majestic grandeur, and the beautiful landscape it commands, words cannot describe'. Beyond the lake St Anne's Hill, Cooper's Hill and Windsor could be seen on one side, and Walton Bridge, Sunbury, Harrow and Highgate on the other. It was commonly reported that Oatlands was more notable for its external views than for its internal scenery, although the latter included the astonishing two-storey grotto (Fig 12.1; now gone).

Fig 12.1
Grotto at Oatlands. [Print from
***Ladies Magazine*, pre-1788]**

The straight walk did not vanish altogether, however, and could provide long-range views while remaining regular in itself. At Goldney, Bristol, Thomas Goldney III, businessman, merchant and Quaker, constructed a garden in mid-century that was surprisingly formal for its date, but where versatile use was made of the terrace walk. There were in fact two, one above the elaborate grotto, terminating the south end of the principal lawn and canal, and this sat above an open paddock. It was gravelled and contained statuary and was completed in 1755 (Fig 12.2). But the more remarkable is a slightly earlier bastion walk, projecting westwards and built up in the manner of a fortification. This terminated in a round bastion, as seems was the case at Oatlands. Although at a lower level than the terrace, the grassed bastion walk stood at some height above the ground, which fell away below (Fig 12.3). Vines were planted on the south side of the substantial walls, and a good view was obtained of the Bristol Channel and Goldney's ships coming into port.

Even at the end of the century straight walks could still be created. At Polesden Lacey 'Sheridan's Walk' (Fig 12.4), with a stone wall and a number of bays and seats along it, marches along in formal style, looking out over a relatively gentle slope and tame Surrey woods. Repton was keen on the terrace for the views it afforded, whether it had to be created or an existing feature could be exploited as at Kenwood.

Fig 12.2
Straight terrace walk at Goldney.

Fig 12.3 (right)
Bastion walk at Goldney.

Fig 12.4 (far right)
Sheridan's Walk at Polesden Lacey.

Fig 12.5
Terrace walk at Castle Howard.
[Source Historic England Archive
CC52/00653]

Fig 12.5
Terrace walk at Castle Howard.
[Source Historic England Archive
CC52/00653]

Fig 12.6
Ionic temple and walk at
Duncombe Park. [© Historic
England Archive DP027576]

Conversely, the early terrace walk at Castle Howard was a curve, at a time when regularity ruled in most of the gardens there (as indeed elsewhere). The walk, affording views across the south lake and to the landscape beyond, followed the line of the old Henderskelfe village street and thus conformed to the existing contours rather than imposing a line on them (Fig 12.5).

A pair of the most dramatic terrace walks is to be found in North Yorkshire. The earlier was Duncombe Park, but it is not known for sure who was the designer of the grounds *c* 1715–20. Vanbrugh was working at Castle Howard not far away, and the Ionic Temple is attributed to him, an open rotunda similar to his construction at Stowe. The principal feature is the half-mile East Terrace, a broad, curving grassed walk with the Ionic Temple at one end (Fig 12.6) and the Doric Temple, attributed to Sir Thomas Robinson, at the other, with a sundial statue by Van Nost en route. The terrace is built up, as the serpentine wall behind reveals, forming a half ha-ha, and looks down upon the River Wye some way below, although now the outward views are much occluded by trees. At the Doric Temple the walk turns virtually 90 degrees to become the South Terrace, equally with views down the steep slope to the river, which has swung right round in the valley. This walk is, however, nearly straight.

In retrospect, Duncombe Park seems something like a dummy run for the even more striking Rievaulx Terrace, composed by Thomas Duncombe III, grandson of the founder of Duncombe Park three miles away. It appears that there may even have been a project to link the two properties. Rievaulx Terrace echoed Duncombe structurally in consisting of a curving half-mile stretch of turf above a drop, with a temple at each end, but the walk is broader and is actually a flat shelf cut out of the top of the hillside (Fig 12.7). What is different is the panorama of scenery that the terrace provides – in the distance Yorkshire hills and in the middle distance, looking down, the valley floor with the ruins of the Cistercian Rievaulx Abbey. Not only is the scenery on a wider scale but the way of seeing it is controlled, which in 1718 would not have been thought of, whereas 40 years later the 'picturesque' sensibility was keenly attuned to the idea of presenting framed views or pictures. To this end 13 distinct viewing points were cut through the trees and bushes on the slope beneath the terrace so that, as one walked along, a series of vistas from different angles presented themselves in the valley. Some were of rural scenery generally (farmhouse, bridge), but most were of the Abbey, showing it from a startling spectrum of aspects (Fig 12.8).

Fig 12.7
Rievaulx Terrace.

Fig 12.8
View of abbey from Rievaulx
Terrace. [© Historic England
Archive DP169245]

While the majority of visitors, then and ever since, have admired the arrangement of views from the Rievaulx Terrace, nonetheless there have been some who preferred to view the Abbey from the valley floor – being closer it had more immediate and emotional impact, and was seen as more 'romantic' than from the detached distance and elevation of the terrace. Such visitors even disparaged the distant views from the terrace.

A third example in North Yorkshire, much lesser known, is the terrace at Kirkby Fleetham. Owned by William Aislabie of Studley Royal and Hackfall, the terrace itself, named as such on maps, followed the course of the river below while the walk wound within a wood, sometimes emerging, and was marked by summer houses at strategic points.

Another example of a terrace walk that dominates the garden is at Farnborough Hall, Warwickshire, in existence by 1742. While level in itself, the broad grass avenue reaches up and round, along a ridge overlooking a considerable valley and plain across to the Malvern Hills. It extends a full three-quarters of a mile from the house (Fig 12.9), terminating at an obelisk. Along the outward-facing edge is a hedge punctuated by bays, bastions that accord with the Edge Hill site of the Civil War they look out to (now unfortunately bisected by the M40). Set into the hill, below the walk, is an Ionic Temple by Sanderson Miller, who was also responsible for the miniature Oval Pavilion further along the way. The decoration of the upper room is pure rococo, by the same *stuccadore* who worked in the house. Off the track, to one side, is Miller's hexagonal game larder, at once functional and ornamental.

Fig 12.9
Walk with bays at Farnborough Hall.

13 | 'Capability' Brown and the Brownians

Lancelot 'Capability' Brown was the indisputable giant of the landscape garden and the only name familiar to the general public. His achievements were formidable, and the sheer number of his commissions (well over 200), meant that he stood apart from all others in terms of spreading taste and fostering the fashion for his particular vision of what a landscape garden should be. So influential was he that it is no exaggeration to say, as has often been claimed, that he transformed the face of the English countryside, with many followers working broadly in his style.

The characteristics of a Brown landscape are well known – rolling grass slopes, dips and swells, a lake in the middle ground, trees dotted about singly or in clumps (often on a hill), a perimeter belt of woodland containing a ride, and above all long and expansive views. Brown made copious use of the ha-ha, which enabled him to bring lawn right up to the house, in effect merging park and garden. He had particular strengths, such as water engineering, which permitted him to undertake ambitious water schemes that would be practical as well as aesthetic. Although he is sometimes regarded as being formulaic in approach, that does not take into account his uncanny eye for views. This has been illustrated recently at Belvoir Castle, Leicestershire, where his plan was not executed at the time, but after its discovery it was decided to implement it from 2015. What was found in the process was how astutely Brown had placed trees so as to obtain the maximum from long views – a single tree in the wrong place could utterly spoil such a view.

Brown has often been characterised as the creator of abstract, even minimalist, parks, but there are built structures in many of his landscapes, often in the form of a bridge but also eye-catcher follies, designed either by Brown himself or by other architects. In some cases the building forms a key focal point in the scene, as at Wimpole, where Brown adapted Sanderson Miller's original design for the ruined castle (Fig 13.1). Brown's style changed and developed: the earliest of his independent commissions, Croome Court (from 1751), shows him working to some extent in the pictorial idiom reminiscent of nearby Stourhead, with a circuit punctuated by plantings, buildings and shrubberies as at Stowe. Another early work was Wotton, Buckinghamshire (Fig 13.2).

Fig 13.1
Ruined castle at Wimpole.
[© Michael Cousins]

Brown was certainly brought in for the practical matter of water management, but the layout, a circuit leading from one building to another, with views across the lake, owes much to Stowe, which was from 1750 the seat of Richard Grenville, brother of George Grenville of Wotton. A number of authors have pointed out that Brown's early work often includes buildings, regular plantations, rococo elements and a concentration on decoration in the pleasure grounds near the house. Later there was more emphasis on the simplicity of a park.

The tercentenary year of Brown's birth (2016) saw a great many celebrations, publications and the products of new research and thinking about Brown. There were also two inventories of sites where Brown either definitely or possibly worked, but they do not usually indicate the proportion or extent of Brown's input or achievement, which in some cases might have been slight. He may have been brought in for some specific project, such as work on a lake, rather than designing the gardens as a whole. Obviously the existence of a Brown plan confirms his (re)design of part or whole of a site, but the questions then follow: (a) how far did the owner influence the plan, (b) how far was it implemented and (c) was it modified by others? Harewood House, Yorkshire, would be a good case in point. Brown was commissioned to produce a plan in 1758, but it is known that other designers rapidly came on the scene – Richard Woods, Anthony Sparrow and Thomas White in the 1760s, to be followed later by John Webb, Adam Mickle (1790) and finally Repton (1800). Who could possibly claim today that one is looking out over a Brown landscape? Or at Bowood, Wiltshire, hailed as one of Brown's masterpieces, where Jeremy Bentham, staying there in 1781, maintained that the retired Charles Hamilton of Painshill had 'been employ'd in undoing what Capability Brown had done'.

The connection with the surrounding countryside is of particular interest. As has been said, the frequent perimeter belt of trees denoted the limits of the estate, so any views beyond were clearly of distant scenery that was not part of the designed park. But some estates on which Brown worked were so vast that they would fill all, or most, of the view and would contain, as part of the plan, agricultural areas that would resemble countryside, hence the claim that he transformed the face of the countryside. This has also led to suggestions that, when pasture was decorated with trees, the estate should be regarded as a *ferme ornée*.

The difference between Brown and the pictorial style can be illustrated most vividly by their juxtaposition at Kew. Kew proper was, as noted in Chapter 9, a circuit punctuated by a large number of buildings around open fields and a lake. Richmond Gardens, the other half of the present Kew Gardens (the two were not united until 1802), had until 1764 been a Kentian circuit with several buildings in addition to the Hermitage and Merlin's Cave, and to some extent resembled Kew in style. All that changed radically, however, after Brown became Royal Gardener. He reduced the formal riverside terrace to a natural lawn at ground level, dismantled the revetment wall of the terrace, varied the flat site by excavating a hollow (now the Rhododendron Dell) and knocked down the Hermitage and Merlin's Cave. Landscaping replaced iconography and residual formality (Fig 13.3). In Kew itself, on the other hand, the number of buildings swelled in the 1760s, under William Chambers, and the gardens took the pictorial direction.

Fig 13.3
Informality at Kew in foreground, looking across the Thames to Syon House, also landscaped by Brown. Aquatint after Joseph Farington. [© British Library Board (192.f.9 p030)]

Fig 13.4
Lake and bridge at Blenheim.
[© Historic England Archive
AA98/06 110]

Fig 13.5
Cascade at Blenheim.
[© Michael Cousins]

Brown's masterpiece is generally reckoned to be Blenheim, where he constructed a lake in place of a miserable canal that did no justice to Vanbrugh's imposing bridge. By submerging the lower part of the bridge and surrounding it by water (Fig 13.4), Brown brought bridge and water into perfect balance. With reference to his aqueous effects at Blenheim, which included a cascade (Fig 13.5), Brown is said to have exclaimed, 'Thames, Thames, will you ever forgive me?' There was far more to Brown's work than the lake, however, and his landscaping included an extensive lawn directly in front of the south front of the Palace, much planting and judicious locating of trees on the lake banks to permit framed views of the Palace and lake. But in the end it was the combination of Brown's lake and the pre-existing bridge that produced such a memorable and iconic picture.

It is difficult to pick out just a few of the most outstanding Brown parks, which would suggest a ranking of quality, but Petworth, Sussex, would be near the top of most lists (Fig 13.6). Although the extensive parkland, with its clumps on hills and its areas for deer, is the most apparent of its charms, Brown also designed the pleasure grounds near the house, with shrubberies, flowers and a small open temple. For the serenity of an English country house setting in summer, Compton Verney, Warwickshire, would be hard to beat (Fig 13.7); likewise Ugbrooke in Devon (Fig 13.8). Most, of course, depended on the local terrain, so the park at Alnwick,

Fig 13.6
Petworth lake and park.
Early 19th-century print.

Fig 13.7 (below)
Bridge and lake at Compton Verney.

Fig 13.8 (below right)
Lake at Ugbrooke.

Northumberland, is suitably rugged, while the plunging combe at Prior Park, Avon, brings the city of Bath, in all its elegance, into the picture (Fig 13.9). Burghley, Lincolnshire, had various historicist elements taken out into the park, while at Claremont Brown had the opportunity to naturalise further the landscaping carried out by Kent, as well as building a neo-Palladian house for Lord Clive. At Scampston, Yorkshire, he designed a beautiful Palladian bridge (Fig 13.10) in the manner of Robert Adam, as well as landscaping the grounds and creating two cascades, one in the body of the lake and the other just behind his bridge.

It is unfair to classify the so-called Brownians as a single group working in the style of the master. While in some cases producing plodding, formulaic plans lacking inspiration, and incurring the wrath of Uvedale Price and Richard Payne Knight, who disparaged the 'tasteless herd' of Brown's followers, nonetheless the best of them had specialisms and individuality. Some worked widely over the country, like Richard Woods, especially good at pleasure grounds; others, like Thomas White, father and son, and Adam Mickle (three generations), worked regionally, in their case in the north. Some had actually worked under Brown, such as Thomas Cook (West Wycombe), William Gould (who went out to Russia to create a number of landscapes for Prince Potemkin) and Samuel Lapidge (Chiswick and elsewhere). But as a totality they were all helping to spread the taste for simplicity and naturalistic park-making.

Fig 13.9
View of Bath from Prior Park.
[© National Trust Images/
James Dobson]

Fig 13.10
Palladian bridge at Scampston.

14 | The Picturesque and Sublime

William Gilpin, pioneer of the Picturesque, attempted to define what he meant by the word in *An Essay upon Prints* (1768): 'a term expressive of that peculiar kind of beauty, which is agreeable in a picture'. If only he had left it at such a simple concept, future commentators would have been spared much perplexity. Unfortunately his own predilection for the mountainous scenery of his native Lake District led him to refine – and confine – what he regarded as suitable for a picture as that wilder sort of landscape – untamed, rugged, uneven surfaces, broken, irregular. This, for example, led him to assert that no regular building could be picturesque, only an uneven ruin. Even where he depicted cattle in his sketches, they had to be in odd numbers, preferably three, because an even number would not be picturesque (Repton did the same). When the concept of the Picturesque spread in France there were no such restrictions, and the art of the garden designer was closely allied with that of the landscape painter, sometimes to the extent of the same artist combining both activities, such as Hubert Robert.

The notion of a Wild Picturesque led unerringly to Uvedale Price and, more especially, Richard Payne Knight in the 1790s, advocating that art should be employed as little as possible and that the landscape should look totally natural and untouched. Where art was found to be necessary (as in both their estates), the results should look natural – Price was fond of quoting 'the art that conceals art'.

A further dimension that has caused confusion was Price's attempt to locate the Picturesque as a category between the Beautiful and the Sublime, moving towards the latter. The Sublime, as enunciated by Edmund Burke and others, was, in landscape terms, the terrifying, the vast and the precipitous. Mountains, rocks, chasms and dramatic waterfalls would furnish the sort of experience that could be classified as sublime. But purely as an aesthetic category the Picturesque thereby ceases to have any direct or necessary connection with paintings. For examination of this and other strands of the Picturesque the reader is referred to the present author's *The Picturesque and the Later Georgian Garden*.

The picturesque garden grew, as we have seen, from the mid-18th-century pictorial landscape, presenting a series of scenes or views, usually in a circuit. Buildings decreased in number, to be replaced by natural features or those that sought an emotional response. The print in Fig 14.1 (1753), a waterfall in Bolton Park, North Yorkshire, displays a natural

Fig 14.1

Cascade at Bolton Park, drawn and engraved by François Vivares, 1753.

feature which has been 'enhanced' by a viewing path and plantings. It is described in the caption as 'a Beautiful & Romantic Natural cascade', thus playing on the viewer's imagination and feelings. This is demonstrated by the visitors' efforts to negotiate the rocks.

A number of components could be found, in varying degrees, in a picturesque garden. One was the outward view, which might contribute enormously, as in the views out to sea and across the Plymouth Sound at Mount Edgcumbe, just on the Cornish side of the Devon/Cornwall border (Fig 14.2). A view of distant mountains might colour the experience of the garden, as with the West Midlands trio of Enville, Hagley and The Leasowes, all looking westwards to Wales.

Fig 14.2
Sea view from Mount Edgcumbe, drawn and engraved by William Daniell, 1825.

Fig 14.3
Alpine bridge at Hawkstone.

Buildings, even if in declining numbers, could still provide focal points of interest, especially those that bore a direct relation to the Picturesque. One category was ruins, either genuine or sham (purpose-built), which suited the Gilpin school by their visual irregularity and also by the emotional effect they produced, predominantly a melancholy in looking back on the passing and disintegration of bygone times. The other was rustic architecture, often constructed of the sort of materials that might be found in the landscape around, and which would accord with simplicity and naturalness. Hermitages, rustic huts and simple (sometimes perilous) bridges were characteristic. The dangerous appearance of a bridge would produce the appropriate sublime frisson, as with the 'Alpine bridge' spanning a ravine at Hawkstone (Fig 14.3).

Another pronounced feature of many picturesque landscapes was rockwork. As time went on, that would increasingly mean natural rocks *in situ* forming cascades, outcrops or cliffs. Their picturesque effect could be enhanced by plantings or viewing points. But it also meant the use of rocks to form, above all, grottoes of a natural, cave-like appearance. This kind of creation proliferated from mid-18th-century and, although the exterior might be plain and cave-like, the interior could be dazzling in decoration, usually in a combination of shells and minerals arranged in patterns or as crystal stalactites. As we have seen, such intensive decoration died down, especially under Josiah Lane, whose later work included the starker or cyclopean structures at Wardour (Fig 14.4), Bowood and Fonthill.

Fig 14.4
Grotto at Wardour.
[© Historic England Archive
DP083089/93]

In the case of plantings, variety of patterns (sometimes of form or colour) and irregularity of density and placing were vital, as was an emphasis on indigenous trees, because that would accord with the illusion that they grew there 'naturally'. Walpole wrote in 1770 of a category of forest or savage garden that, while originating in Switzer, portrayed the picturesque effect of dense woodland: 'I mean that kind of alpine scene, composed almost wholly of pines and firs, a few birch, and such trees as assimilate with a savage and mountainous country.' His exemplar was the 'forest' at the western end of Painshill.

Fig 14.5
View of Wyndcliffe from Piercefield.
Print by J Newman, 1842.

Fig 14.6
Quarry garden at Belsay.
[© Historic England Archive
DP034840]

Some gardens, such as Stourhead and Painshill, were laid out in the pictorial circuit style but responded to picturesque taste. An originally predominantly classical circuit at Stourhead was later expanded and modified by the addition of exotica like the Chinese Umbrello and the Turkish Tent, together with the rustic cottage by the lake and the Gothic convent in the woods, and particularly the primitive tree-branch Hermitage at a bend in the steep path up to the Temple of Apollo. The Hermitage was placed according to the advice of Charles Hamilton of Painshill. Hamilton himself, always eclectic in his array of buildings, took advantage of varied landform and introduced rockwork – the most stupendous of grottoes and a cascade – in addition to his final picturesque touch, the Ruined Abbey.

Among picturesque landscapes – the word 'romantic' was often used to describe them at the time – Piercefield, Mount Edgcumbe, Belsay and Plumpton Rocks stand out, although there are many more examples. Piercefield, near Chepstow, was famed more for its views outside than internally, ranging from the River Severn in the distance to the ruined Chepstow Castle and, especially, the Wyndcliffe, a mixture of bare rock and vegetation (Fig 14.5). The scene looks today much as it did at the time. There was no shortage of excitement within the grounds either, with the vertiginous Lover's Leap and a cave guarded by the stone figure of a giant holding a threatening rock.

Mount Edgcumbe was founded on hilly terrain, but the chief attraction was the views obtainable from various points and in different directions – the sea to the south (*see* Fig 14.2), Plymouth Sound and the docks to the east, the Tamar and beyond it the moors to the north. The naval activity in the Sound contributed to the picturesque effect, Lady Edgcumbe writing in 1778: 'You have no idea what an amazing sight it is, 30 sail of line now lying under a terrace of shrubs as if only to ornament our Park!'

The centrepiece of Belsay, Northumberland, is the quarry garden (Fig 14.6), with the tall rock faces forming a protected walled garden *par excellence*. That dates from the early 19th century, but the landscape had been laid out in pictorial form from 1764, including the crenellated Bantam Folly.

Plumpton Rocks near Harrogate (Fig 14.7) is the ultimate picturesque garden, consisting as it does of some massive and bizarre rock formations of millstone grit that were flooded by an artificial although natural-looking lake, and ornamented by plantings of flowers and shrubs, together with woodland. The principal rock was grassed over, as were some of the others, and planted up as a minute garden with flowers. As at Piercefield, Brimham Rocks and other places, there was a Lover's Leap at Plumpton (Fig 14.8), the romantic connotations of which echoed through the Victorian era and beyond.

Fig 14.7
Plumpton Rocks.

Fig 14.8
Lover's Leap, Plumpton Rocks.

The three leading sublime gardens were Hafod, Hackfall and Hawkstone. The gardens mentioned above were all nudging in the direction of the Sublime, but lacked the sense of danger inherent in this trio, although the Lover's Leap at Piercefield and at Plumpton Rocks were frightening enough. Hafod, in mid-Wales, was in a bleak spot amid largely bare mountains when Thomas Johnes inherited it in 1780. He planted on a massive scale and created a number of sublime effects, such as a perilous rustic bridge (Johnes said he intended to scare the visitor even to death), augmenting the natural Peiran Falls (Fig 14.9) and fashioning the Cavern Cascade, a fall thundering down an enclosed shaft and accessed by a reverberating tunnel. Hafod had two flower gardens at an upper level, and Johnes is said to have worked with William Mason's poem *The English Garden* in hand. Johnes was cousin to Richard Payne Knight and a friend of Price, in addition to being brought up in the romantic surroundings of Croft Castle, Herefordshire, and thus was thoroughly steeped in the Picturesque, although some developments at Hafod predated the defining publications of 1794.

Hackfall, North Yorkshire, was developed by William Aislabie of Studley Royal between 1749 and 1767. In contrast to the smooth, cool perfection of his father's water gardens at Studley, Aislabie pursued a wild naturalism in a site that expressed the Picturesque and Sublime perfectly. Paths under steep rock faces, two long glens marching down to the turbulent River Ure, ubiquitous streams and cascades that climaxed with the Forty-Foot Fall (Fig 14.10), all contributed to the excitement. Nature was given a helping hand, for example by the addition of shelves of stone to enhance the Forty-Foot Fall, but by and large it was the steepness of the site and the natural features that made it sublime. A number of follies formed focal points in the view, such as the (mock) ruined Mowbray Castle, Mowbray Point (classical from the front, Gothic from the rear) and the alum-covered Fisher's Hall.

Hawkstone, north-east Shropshire, contained the geological freak of sandstone cliffs that suddenly stand up 300 feet from the surrounding predominantly flat country. The Sublime of Hawkstone revolved around these cliffs – vertiginous narrow paths, precipices and dizzying heights. Dr Johnson was terrified to go back the way he came, cowering before 'the extent of its prospects, the awfulness of its shades, the horrors of its precipices, the verdure of its hollows and the loftiness of its rocks. The ideas which it forces upon the mind, are the sublime, the dreadful, and the vast. Above, is inaccessible altitude, below is horrible profundity'. There was a great deal of variety at Hawkstone, varying from the hermitage with live hermit (or mechanical successor) to the vineyard with

Fig 14.9

Peiran Falls at Hafod.

Fig 14.10
Forty-Foot Fall at Hackfall, engraved
by J Rogers after N Whittock, 1830.

Fig 14.11
Cleft at Hawkstone.

bastion and towers, the Cleft (a gigantic fissure in the rock some hundred metres long, Fig 14.11), a Dutch windmill, a 'scene in Otaheite', a Gothic greenhouse, and, as we have seen, numerous moral inscriptions along the circuit.

It might be added that neglect (sometimes deliberate), combined with the natural growth of trees and other vegetation by the late 18th century, rendered many earlier gardens, even those with elements surviving from the baroque era, more picturesque than originally envisaged. Accidental Picturesque may well affect the reactions of a visitor in this late period, just as images from that time may present a misleading picture to present-day readers or viewers.

15 | Repton and a new direction

Humphry Repton is often seen as the successor to Brown, but that did not mean that he copied Brown to any great extent or that he lacked his own individuality of style. Sometimes he worked on an estate previously laid out by Brown (for example, Harewood or Longleat), which would leave little scope except to modify Brown's plantings. But even if he followed broadly in Brown's footsteps, Repton was inevitably influenced by the Picturesque, arguments about which came to a head in the mid-1790s, when Repton was only a few years into his practice as a landscape gardener.

Repton came relatively late to gardens, after reaching a crisis point in his life in 1788, at the age of 36. There were no outstanding practitioners at the time, and Repton sensed a gap. He set himself up as a 'landscape gardener', and his *Prospect* (prospectus) of 1789 announced his credentials on the basis of having long 'studied the picturesque effect resulting from the art of LAYING OUT GROUND'. Art was the essential word: when it came to his own practice, Repton proclaimed 'Gardens are works of art rather than of nature' (in his designs for the Royal Pavilion at Brighton).

Unlike Brown, Repton put his ideas and theories in substantial written form. Many of these ideas arose in connection with particular estates he was involved with, for the owners of which he would generally produce what has become known as a Red Book. This was an individual, handwritten and hand-produced portfolio usually bound in red Morocco leather, hence the name. It would present Repton's thoughts about the 'capabilities' of the property, together with a beguiling series of watercolours giving views before and after Repton's proposed improvements. This was achieved by means of a flap (Repton called it a slide) which would be lifted to reveal the astonishing – and often unrealistic – intended transformation (Figs 15.1 and 15.2). The Red Books became prized possessions, but more as works of art customised for the owner than as blueprints for actual design. Sadly, it is reckoned that very few proposals were carried out to an extent that would have satisfied

Fig 15.1 (below)
'Before' view of Harlestone, from Humphry Repton, *Fragments on the Theory and Practice of Landscape Gardening*, 1816 (flap down).

Fig 15.2 (below right)
'After' view of Harlestone, from Humphry Repton, *Fragments on the Theory and Practice of Landscape Gardening*, 1816 (flap lifted).
[© The British Library Board (Repton, H 1712 Red Book 441.g.21, plate 6, fig 1)]

Fig 15.3
Vignette from Humphry
Repton, *Observations on the
Theory and Practice of Landscape
Gardening*, 1803.

Repton, and many remained fantasies, with some ideas partly implemented at a later date by other hands.

The vignette reproduced as Fig 15.3 shows clearly the three components of Repton's art and approach to garden improvement: the artist's palette and brushes, the surveying instruments such as the theodolite and the implements of the working gardener. No other landscape designer could have produced the combination of all three, so this single image gives us Repton's distinctiveness, although he left the practical side to others.

The clientele for which Repton worked – progressively more *nouveaux riches* than the old Whig grandees – reflected changes in society and taste and also the generally smaller-scale estates to be improved. Sometimes Repton bemoaned the lack of taste (meaning the taste of a previous generation) of the owner, but he was astute enough to recognise that to get on professionally he had to please the client. He used the term 'convenience' to indicate that the client's comfort came first, and that aesthetic theory had to follow in second place. Not that Repton was short of theory: his Red Books and publications are full of didactic suggestions usually anchored to particular sites but in total forming a more or less coherent philosophy of landscape gardening. Some of his thinking was not particularly original – Repton drew heavily on Whately, for instance.

Repton claimed that he drew up designs for 400 sites (as against Brown's 200 plus), although records such as the Red Books indicate a smaller total. The very fact that the proposals were drawn up in pictorial form rather than as plans demonstrates a much more visual approach, as with Kent, and a desire to create decorative views that would appeal to the client. Iconography gave way to attractive set scenes that can be quite small (such as a Chinese kiosk on top of a rockery at Woburn Abbey) but fitting into an overall scheme (the rockery was in view of the Chinese Dairy). Emphasis on decorative gardening near the house led to flower gardens and sometimes the return of formality to act as contrast to the wilder park outside – a sort of Villa Picturesque.

Flower gardens, as advocated by Repton, were by no means new. Brown and his followers had designed some; William Chambers was responsible for one at Kew which formed the subject of a popular print (*see* Fig 10.1); Thomas Wright and William Mason designed them, the latter at Nuneham Courtenay (*see* Fig 8.4), which Repton had seen, although in an overgrown condition; and Repton went back to models from the earlier formal era as in his *treillage* view of Richmond Lodge. Even his antagonists Price and Knight were in favour of formal layouts near the house, although their idea was Italianate, incorporating sculpture and other stonework, which Repton rejected.

Repton was in something of a quandary in the 1790s. On one hand he saw himself as the champion of Brown, and indeed was moved to defend him on occasion, but on the other he tried to be flexible enough to accommodate the Picturesque, and started the decade in friendship with the fiery Knight and Price. They attacked Brown's use of clumps, which were intended for posterity, unlike

Kent's, whereupon Repton pointed out that the majority of trees involved, especially firs, were only nurses that should be removed (unfortunately this did not always happen): out of 50 or 60 trees, only the tenth in the middle were intended to grow fully. Nevertheless he was not uncritical of Brown, and in his Red Book for Hewell Grange, Worcestershire, where Brown had worked earlier, he identified what he considered the five leading defects of 'Brown's System', namely the ha-ha, the circuitous approach to the house, the belt, the clump and bare lawn near the house or on the banks of river or lake. With regard to belts, Repton did not object in principle – in fact he thought them necessary to delineate the extent of an owner's property – but was more guarded in the way they had been executed in the past and he sometimes designed a broken belt for aesthetic effect. He was clearly dismayed by being attacked in 1794 by Knight and Price, who thought he had betrayed the Picturesque by selling out to his clients' wishes. Repton, of course, had to make a living, which the two idealist squires could afford to disregard.

Repton had certain design traits that can be identified. He planted luxuriantly behind a house to act as a backcloth when viewed from the front; he proposed ornamental lakes where there were none, although few were executed; he favoured animation in the view, whether deer, cattle or people, and liked water to stir and move; he made the most of distant views and sought to include signs of habitation in them (the Red Books contain images of cottages in a wood with smoke curling from the chimney); he would vary woodland, thinning or making more dense according to the existing situation; and he aimed at variety, although individual compartments (he called them episodes) demanded consistency, such as his proposal for Chinese plantings to complement the Chinese Dairy at Woburn Abbey. He used the word 'appropriation' to indicate the extent of ownership, and his designs always relate to the house (unlike some of the earlier freestanding circuit gardens). His trade card (Fig 15.4) indicates the sort of landscape he wished to promote: rich planting, right down to the lake; water the central feature, naturalistic in shape; the contrast of open ground; and a tower rising from the trees, an effect he was actually to achieve at Blaise.

Fig 15.4
Repton's trade card,
engraved by Thomas Medland
after Repton, 1788.

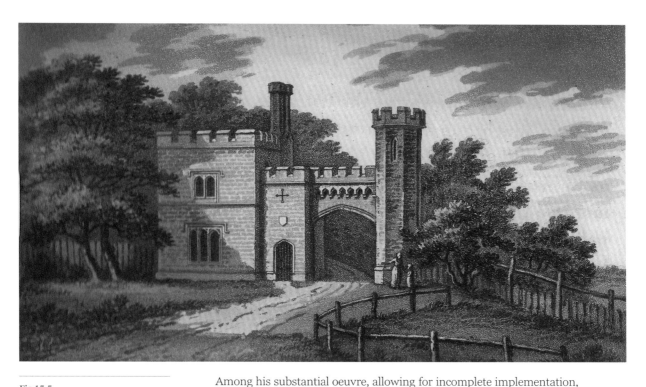

Fig 15.5
Lodge at Blaise, from Humphry
Repton, *Observations on the
Theory and Practice of Landscape
Gardening*, 1803 (flap lifted).

Fig 15.6
Dairy at Blaise.

Among his substantial oeuvre, allowing for incomplete implementation, a few notable surviving or restored commissions may be singled out. Blaise, near Bristol, was a truly picturesque site which Repton made the most of. He designed a castellated lodge (Fig 15.5) that foreshadowed not the house but a sham castle rising from the woods, created back in 1766. The approach looped back and forth, taking in changes of level and passing a thatched timber lodge, a woodland cottage and a deep ravine. In addition, a separate drive took visitors round points of interest while a walk covered such excitements as the Lover's Leap and a cavern opening on a hill across the valley. Nearer the house there was intimate Picturesque with

John Nash's dairy faced with its ornamental pool (Fig 15.6) and the delightful set of *cottages ornés*, each different, that comprises Blaise Hamlet.

Figure 15.7 shows Repton's plan for the series of garden compartments at Ashridge, Hertfordshire, but in practice they were modified and implemented subsequently by Wyatville. The same was true of the dramatic site of Endsleigh, on the Devon/Cornwall border, where the compartments near the house and indeed much of the wider landscaping were modified by Wyatville after Repton's death. The outside views, down to and across the Tamar, were magnificent, and were enjoyed from a broad terrace with a pierced wall on one side (Fig 15.8).

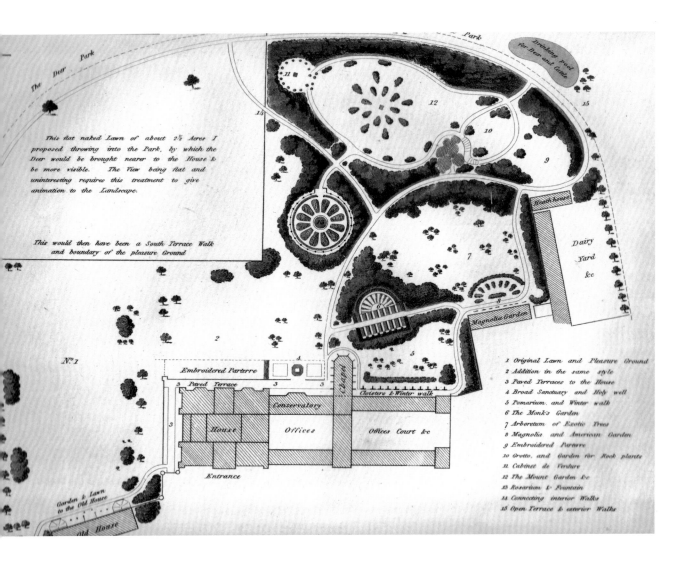

The Deer Park

This flat naked Lawn of about 2½ Acres I proposed throwing into the Park, by which the Deer would be brought nearer to the House & be more visible. The View being flat and uninteresting requires this treatment to give animation to the Landscape.

This would then have been a South Terrace Walk and boundary of the pleasure Ground

No 1

Embroidered Parterre
Paved Terrace
Conservatory
House *Offices* *Offices Court &c*
Cloisters & Winter walk
Entrance
Garden & Lawn to the Old House
Old House

Park
Drinking Pool for Deer and Cattle

Heath house

Dairy Yard &c

Magnolia Garden

1 Original Lawn and Pleasure Ground
2 Addition in the same style
3 Paved Terraces to the House
4 Broad Sanctuary and Holy well
5 Pomarium and Winter walk
6 The Monk's Garden
7 Arboretum of Exotic Trees
8 Magnolia and American Garden
9 Embroidered Parterre
10 Grotto and Garden for Rock plants
11 Cabinet de Verdure
12 The Mount Garden &c
13 Rosarium & Fountain
14 Connecting interior Walks
15 Open Terrace & exterior Walks

Fig 15.7
Plan for gardens near house at Ashridge, from Humphry Repton, *Fragments on the Theory and Practice of Landscape Gardening*, 1816.

At Woburn Abbey Repton was called in by the 6th Duke of Bedford in 1804 to complete, and in some places to amend, work already undertaken by Henry Holland, who had been responsible for buildings such as the Chinese Dairy and for several plantations. Repton's contributions were two-fold – to prettify and ornament the pleasure grounds around the Abbey and, further out, to construct such special features as the Thornery, a cottage surrounded by a collection of all available types of thorn. Among recently restored features is the Chinese kiosk mentioned above (Fig 15.9).

Repton took the idea of a garden area complementing a building in an Indian direction at Sezincote, Gloucestershire. There the thornery comprised the Indian-style garden with a bridge with Brahminee bulls (Fig 15.10), a column with a serpent coiled round it and a temple to the god Souriya, all to match the unusual Indian architecture of the house, which inspired the Royal Pavilion at Brighton.

Fig 15.8
Pierced wall and terrace
at Endsleigh.

Fig 15.9 (above)
Chinese kiosk and rockery
at Woburn Abbey.

Fig 15.10 (above right)
Brahminee bull bridge at Sezincote.

At the opposite extreme, Repton worked at a few estates, such as Holkham and Sheringham in Norfolk, where a distant view of the sea was to be obtained: he warned, however, that being north-facing they took the wind straight from the North Sea, as opposed to the warm properties on the south coast, including the Isle of Wight. Overall, Repton, although progressively concentrating on the ornamental (and sometimes whimsical) near the house, was a landscapist fully aware of, and responsive to, the requirements of long views.

16 Legacy

The effects of the landscape garden have been felt ever since its inception, and can be identified today with what is regarded as attractive parkland or even countryside. Furthermore, a number of modern designers still use some of its elements and principles and endorse its ecology and land management. It is partly a matter of taste, inasmuch as walks in the country or across wilder landscape owe their appeal in some measure to the designed landscape garden showing how alluring a landscape could be, both viewed from afar and experienced close at hand.

The best legacy is the original gardens themselves, a large number of which thrive and can be visited. The more spacious gardens have tended to survive, some in the same families. In such cases much of the original layout has remained, including old trees. Much timber is now over-mature, but it must be remembered that the 18th century planted for posterity, and at the time most of the planting would have looked decidedly young. With its balance between agriculture and aesthetics, the format of these gardens has not been perceived to need change, and indeed where there has been change the general move towards restoration and recreation has seen much reinstatement of the original. The commercial demands of estate upkeep, however, have often dictated the incorporation of attractions that will appeal to, and encourage, the modern visitor, ranging from the fairground features at Alton Towers to the safari park at Longleat. Sometimes 18th-century parks have been used as settings for display of sculpture (for example, the Yorkshire Sculpture Park at Bretton) or other installations, thereby giving the gardens a new role (Fig 16.1).

Fig 16.1
Yorkshire Sculpture Park at Bretton.

Legacy itself falls into two categories, one the immediate influence of the landscape garden and the other what we owe to it, or gain from it, today. From a historical perspective, the principal influence both in the UK and abroad seems to have been in the concept of the park, particularly public parks, composed along naturalistic lines and incorporating aspects of the countryside. The prolific garden writer, theorist and designer J C Loudon had much to do with the transition of the (usually private) Brownian park to the public parks of the 19th century, shifting the emphasis towards functionality, public usage and convenience and, often, botanical interest. Early in the century Loudon criticised Repton but by 1840, when he edited Repton's works, he had swung round to admit there were merits in the Reptonian idea of a landscape garden.

One factor that shaped the direction of the influence of the landscape garden was the staying power of the plain Brownian park in comparison with its more adorned and intricate rivals. There is plenty of evidence to show that the pictorial/picturesque gardens that had reached their prime in the mid-18th century sometimes degenerated at an alarming rate: William Marshall visited Enville, Hagley and The Leasowes in 1785 and remarked that they had already become 'seedy' and neglected. By the 1830s many such gardens had either disappeared or become unrecognisable, dependent as they so often were on their creator's vision. The simpler to maintain Brown-style landscape, however, proved longer-lasting, and the 'natural' look did not go out of fashion, even though Brown himself was sometimes attacked.

The wilder Picturesque, however, changed sensibilities for ever, and the tourism to hilly or mountainous regions like the Lake District that is so widespread today indicates a taste that was largely instilled and developed in the second half of the 18th century.

The 19th century saw a halt in the creation of Brownian parks per se (too old-fashioned and not much scope), but a translation of naturalistic layout to public parks began to emerge. Although there were often flower beds and straight or circular paths, there was also much freedom of line and contouring, together with spacious lawns. It was, however, a tame nature, polished and idealised as Brown had done. Elements of botanical interest and instruction might be added: Loudon's Derby Arboretum (1840) was educational as well as aesthetically attractive, labelling the trees and in effect providing lessons in botany and geography. Sometimes the naturalistic areas could be extensive and incorporated playing fields, and in other cases the lawns could be quite small, but with varied planting, as in some of the London squares (for instance, Ladbroke Square, Fig 16.2). Public parks have always been recognised as health-giving, just as landscape gardens, even if unspoken as such, have been.

During the 19th century the 'English garden' became a recognised and named style, along with Dutch,

Fig 16.2
Ladbroke Square, London.

French and Italian styles, although there was difference of opinion as to definitions. The Italianate 'Avenue gardens' towards the south of Regent's Park were contrasted with the contiguous 'English garden', as we can still see, characterised by gentle undulations in the lawns and irregular plantings.

The *fabriques* of the pictorial circuit garden fell out of fashion in Victorian times, to the extent that in 1876 J Thorne dismissed the carefully designed landscape of Painshill: 'It is needless to remark that so elaborately artificial a construction of natural scenery was a mistake in taste.' Subsequent generations have not perceived such gardens as deficient in taste but view them partly as historical artworks and value them in terms of architectural interest.

While suburban gardens, especially at the promptings of the Loudons, and the return of an Italianate formality, militated against the Brown look, there were some instances where an 18th-century sensibility was clearly still at work. An early example, if late for the landscape garden, was Alton Towers, Staffordshire (from 1827), composed along picturesque lines but incorporating up-to-date materials (Fig 16.3) and a rather overblown romanticism that included a blind Welsh harpist. Later came the celebrated Westonbirt House gardens, Gloucestershire (from *c* 1840), where R S Holford showed himself to be a man born a century after his time. He moved the village out of sight, as had been done at Milton Abbas and Nuneham Courtenay; all that he could see from the house was his own property, including park, farmland and the arboretum; the fields were dotted with specimen trees, as was the park; the plantings were richly varied and included the latest introductions such as the Wellingtonia and the monkey puzzle; and the gardens, divided as they were into formal and more naturalistic spaces (Fig 16.4), revealed open lawns and more scattered plantings in the western parts, together with a lake that could not be seen all at once, thereby satisfying 18th-century principles; a ha-ha separated the gardens from the fields to the south.

The so-called 'Brownian tradition' appears to be a relatively recent concept, stemming from Dorothy Stroud's resuscitation of Brown. In 1840, reflecting with hindsight on the landscape movement, Loudon divided it into the bare, smooth and simple, which he called the Kent School (giving Kent rather than Brown the credit for introducing it); the Picturesque School, which took an alternative route of 'roughness and intricacy'; and the Repton School, which combined the best of both schools with good sense and taste.

Fig 16.3
Pagoda at Alton Towers.
[© Michael Cousins]

Fig 16.4
Lawn at Westonbirt House.

In modern times a balance between formal compartments near the house and a more natural look away from it has been achieved even on a small scale. The five hectares at Winfield House, Regent's Park, the second largest private garden in London, contain an extensive sloping lawn bordered by a belt of magnificent trees that block out all sign of the metropolis – truly a *rus in urbe*. The lawn was basically established in the 19th century as part of Regent's Park, but the compartments round the mansion are modern and reflect an architectural approach.

In the end, the landscape garden taught people how to see and enjoy their surroundings, looking ever outwards. Nature is the fundamental appeal, and a landscape garden enables the visitor to engage with it either close up or at a distance. What distinguishes a landscape garden from a completely natural landscape is that it is nature arranged, selected and disposed according to aesthetic criteria, meaning that the eye is pleased. This may admit art in the form of built structures, which in turn add extra dimensions of interest and reward. Above all the landscape garden channels and reflects the glory of the English countryside.

Bibliography

Original published texts

Chambers, W 1757 *Designs of Chinese Buildings ... to which is annexed, a Description of their Temples, Houses, Gardens, &c.* London: Author

Chambers, W 1772 *A Dissertation on Oriental Gardening.* London: W Griffin

Combe, W 1812 *The Tour of Dr. Syntax in Search of the Picturesque, a Poem.* London: R Ackermann

Cradock, J 1775 *Village Memoirs.* London and Dublin: Author

Cumberland, G 1796 *An Attempt to Describe Hafod.* London: T Egerton

Dalrymple, J 1823 [orig. *c* 1760] *An Essay on Landscape Gardening.* London: Bolton Corney

(Gilpin, W) 1748 *A Dialogue upon the Gardens ... at Stow.* Buckingham: B Seeley

Gilpin, W 1782 *Observations on the River Wye, and several parts of South Wales, &c ...* London: R Blamire

Gilpin, W 1786 *Observations ... Made in the Year 1772, on Several Parts of England, particularly the Mountains, and Lakes of Cumberland and Westmoreland.* London: R Blamire

Gilpin, W 1789 *Observations ... Made in the Year 1776, on Several Parts of Great Britain, particularly the Highlands of Scotland.* London: R Blamire

Gilpin, W 1791 *Remarks on Forest Scenery and other Woodland Views ...* London: R Blamire

Gilpin, W 1792 *Three Essays: On Picturesque Beauty; On Picturesque Travel; and on Sketching Landscape.* London: printed for R Blamire, in the Strand

Knight, R P 1794 [revised 1795] *The Landscape: A Didactic Poem.* London: W Bulmer

Malthus, D 1783 *An Essay on Landscape*, translated from the French. London: J Dodsley

Marshall, W 1785 *Planting and Ornamental Gardening: A Practical Treatise.* London: J Dodsley. Reissued 1796 as *On Planting and Rural Ornament*

Mason, G 1768 *An Essay on Design in Gardening.* London: B White. Revised and expanded 1795

Mason, W 1772–81 *The English Garden* [4 vols]. York: printed by A Ward

(Mason, W) 1773 *An Heroic Epistle to Sir William Chambers.* London: J Almon

Matthews, J 1794 *A Sketch from the Landscape.* London: R Faulder

Price, U 1794 *An Essay on the Picturesque.* London: J Robson

Price, U 1798 *Essays on the Picturesque.* London: J Robson

Price, U 1801 *A Dialogue on the Distinct Characters of the Picturesque and the Beautiful.* London: printed by D Walker for J Robson

Repton, H 1794 *Sketches and Hints on Landscape Gardening.* London: J & J Boydell

Repton, H 1803 *Observations on the Theory and Practice of Landscape Gardening.* London: J Taylor

Repton, H 1806 *An Enquiry into the Changes of Taste in Landscape Gardening.* London: J Taylor

Repton, H 1816 *Fragments on the Theory and Practice of Landscape Gardening.* London: J Taylor

(Trusler, J) 1784 *Elements of Modern Gardening.* London: R Baldwin

Whately, T 1770 *Observations on Modern Gardening.* London: T Payne

Young, A 1768 *A Six Weeks Tour Through the Southern Counties of England and Wales.* London: W Nicoll

Young, A 1770 *A Six Months Tour Through the North of England.* London: W Strahan

Modern publications

Bapasola, J 2009 *The Finest View in England: The Landscape and Gardens at Blenheim Palace.* Woodstock: Blenheim Palace

Batey, M 1996 *Jane Austen and the English Landscape.* London: Barn Elms

Batey, M 1999 *Alexander Pope: The Poet and the Landscape.* London: Barn Elms

Bending, S (ed) 2013 *A Cultural History of Gardens, Vol 4: In the Age of Enlightenment.* London: Bloomsbury

Brogden, W A 2017 *Ichnographia Rustica: Stephen Switzer and the Designed Landscape.* Abingdon: Routledge

Brown, D and Williamson, T 2016 *Lancelot Brown and the Capability Men: Landscape Revolution in Eighteenth-Century England.* London: Reaktion Books

Brown, J 2011 *The Omnipotent Magician: Lancelot 'Capability' Brown, 1716–83.* London: Chatto & Windus

Chambers, D D C 1993 *The Planters of the English Landscape Garden: Botany, Trees, and the Georgics.* New Haven: Yale University Press

Clark H F 1948 *The English Landscape Garden.* London: Pleiades Books

Coffin, D 1994 *The English Garden: Meditation and Memorial.* Princeton: Princeton University Press

Cowell, F 2009 *Richard Woods (1715–1793): Master of the Pleasure Garden*. Woodbridge: The Boydell Press

Daniels, S 1999 *Humphry Repton: Landscape Gardening and the Geography of Georgian England*. New Haven: Yale University Press

Davidson, K 2016 *Woburn Abbey: The Parks & Gardens*. London: Pimpernel Press

Desmond, R 1995 *Kew: The History of the Royal Botanic Gardens*. London: Harvill Press

Everett, N 1994 *The Tory View of Landscape*. London and New Haven: Yale University Press

Gemmett, R J 2003 *Beckford's Fonthill: The Rise of a Romantic Icon*. Norwich: Michael Russell

Harris, J 1978 *Gardens of Delight: The Rococo English Landscape of Thomas Robins the Elder* (2 vols). London: Basilisk Press

Harris, J 1994 *The Palladian Revival: Lord Burlington, His Villa and Garden at Chiswick*. New Haven: Yale University Press/ Royal Academy of Arts

Harris, J and Snodin, M 1996 *Sir William Chambers, Architect to George III*. New Haven: Yale University Press/ Courtauld Gallery

Henrey, B 1986 *No ordinary gardener: Thomas Knowlton 1691–1781*. London: British Museum (Natural History)

Hunt, J D 1976 *The Figure in the Landscape: Poetry, Painting, and Gardening during the Eighteenth Century*. Baltimore: The John Hopkins Press

Hunt, J D 1986 *Garden and Grove: The Italian Renaissance Garden in the English Imagination, 1600–1750*. London: J M Dent

Hunt, J D 1987 *William Kent: Landscape Garden Designer*. London: Zwemmer

Hunt, J D 1992 *Gardens and the Picturesque*. Cambridge, MA: MIT Press

Hunt, J D and Willis, P (eds) 1975 *The Genius of the Place: The English Landscape Garden 1620–1820*. London: Paul Elek

Hussey, C 1967 *English Gardens and Landscapes 1700–1750*. London: Country Life

Jacques, D 1983 *Georgian Gardens: The Reign of Nature*. London: Batsford

Jacques, D 2017 *Gardens of Court and Country: English Design, 1630–1730*. New Haven: Yale University Press

Laird, M 1999 *The Flowering of the Landscape Garden: English Pleasure Grounds 1720–1800*. Philadelphia: University of Pennsylvania Press

Laird, M 2015 *A Natural History of English Gardening 1650–1800*. New Haven: Yale University Press

Mowl, T 2000 *Gentlemen & Players: Gardeners of the English Landscape*. Stroud: Sutton Publishing

Newman, M 2015 *The Wonder of the North: Fountains Abbey and Studley Royal*. Woodbridge: The Boydell Press/ National Trust

Phibbs, J 2016 *Capability Brown: Designing the English Landscape*. New York: Rizzoli

Phibbs, J 2017 *Place-making: The art of Capability Brown*. Swindon: Historic England

Richardson, T 2007 *The Arcadian Friends: Inventing the English Landscape Garden*. London: Bantam Press

Ridgway, C and Williams, R 2000 *Sir John Vanbrugh and Landscape Architecture in Baroque England, 1690–1730*. Stroud: Sutton Publishing

Roberts, J 1997 *Royal Landscape: The Gardens and Parks of Windsor*. New Haven: Yale University Press

Robinson, J M 1990 *Temples of Delight: Stowe Landscape Gardens*. London: George Philip/National Trust

Rogger, A 2007 *Landscapes of Taste: The Art of Humphry Repton's Red Books*. Abingdon: Routledge

Rutherford, S 2016 *Capability Brown and his Landscape Gardens*. London: National Trust

Shields, S 2016 *Moving Heaven & Earth: Capability Brown's Gift of Landscape*. London: Unicorn

Stroud, D 1975 *Capability Brown*. London: Faber and Faber

Symes, M 2010 *Mr. Hamilton's Elysium: The Gardens of Painshill*. London: Frances Lincoln

Symes, M 2012 *The Picturesque and the Later Georgian Garden*. Bristol: Redcliffe Press

Symes, M 2016 *The English Landscape Garden in Europe*. Swindon: Historic England

Symes, M (ed) 2016 *Observations on Modern Gardening by Thomas Whately: An Eighteenth-Century Study of the English Landscape Garden*. Woodbridge: The Boydell Press

Symes, M and Haynes, S 2010 *Enville, Hagley, The Leasowes: Three Great Eighteenth-Century Gardens*. Bristol: Redcliffe Press

Watkins, C and Cowell, B 2012 *Uvedale Price (1747–1829): Decoding the Picturesque*. Woodbridge: The Boydell Press

Williamson, T 1995 *Polite Landscapes: Gardens and Society in Eighteenth-Century England*. Stroud: Sutton Publishing

Willis, P 2001 *Charles Bridgeman and the English Landscape Garden*. Newcastle: Elysium Press

The reader is referred also to T Mowl's series of county garden histories for material on 18th-century sites. More specialist reading is to be found in the academic periodicals *Garden History* (journal of The Gardens Trust), *Studies in the History of Designed Landscapes* (formerly *The Journal of Garden History*) and the *New Arcadian Journal*, edited by P Eyres, which contains much exploration of the politics behind 18th-century landscapes. During 2016 several counties published books about Brown and the gardens he designed within that county; likewise 2018 has seen several publications on Repton in separate counties.

Index